Fixed and Free

Praise for *Fixed and Free*

An abecedarian of writers, Albuquerque based and beyond. There are all the local favorites and new voices, a strong mix of page and performance in this inclusive anthology. *Fixed and Free* documents New Mexico as a poetic power point, the secret epicenter of poetry on planet earth. Reading this book you will move from love to love.

—Joan Logghe, Santa Fe Poet Laureate 2010-2012

A mixture of experienced and fledgling poetry voices bring this anthology to life. The poems range from the light-hearted to the tragic and encompass the American landscape from rural to urban settings. You can hear these voices rising like flowers pushing up through the concrete slabs of an ever-harsher America. Read these poems and rejoice in keeping real hope alive for the future.

—Tony Mares, poet

A delicious taste of rich New Mexico diversity from nearly 80 poets. This sampler unfolds from fixed forms to free verse, from slam to spoken word and the printed page, all with a mystery and enchantment to satisfy our hunger.

—Jules Nyquist, author of *Appetites: poems on food, drink and sex (with recipes)*

Albuquerque may be one of the few places where poets of such diverse talents and experience come together simply to share what they love. This anthology is a great core sample of the current Albuquerque scene: honest, profound, and as piercing as the New Mexico sky.

—Mitch Rayes, Albuquerque poet

Leonardo da Vinci wrote, "In order to prove whether the spirit can speak or not, it is necessary in the first place to define what a voice is and how it is generated." In this enchanting gathering of poems, an anthology gleaned from the writers and performers of Albuquerque's long-running "Fixed and Free" live poetry presentations, readers will instantly and repeatedly discover what a voice is and how it is generated. The myriad artists who lend their voices to this volume, many of our finest Southwest poets, prove the spirit can indeed speak, and they articulate sentient spirits on every page. Expect to feel fixed and free!

—Patrick Houlihan, CNM English professor, Watermelon
    Mountain Jug Band singer/songwriter

This is a delightfully diverse collection—linked by a strong sense of place, common to NM poets. The poems give surprising glimpses into both familiar and far away worlds. I want to hear more from these writers. And at the Fixed and Free readings, I can.

—Rachelle Woods, Santa Fe poet

Fixed and Free
poetry for people

Fixed and Free
poetry anthology 2011

Edited by Billy Brown, Gregory L. Candela
Elaine Schwartz and Stewart S. Warren

 Mercury HeartLink

Fixed and Free: poetry anthology 2011
Copyright ©2012 Fixed and Free Poetry

ISBN: 978-0-9827303-3-1
Publisher: Mercury HeartLink

Managing Editor: Billy Brown
Editors: Gregory L. Candela and Elaine Schwartz
Publishing Editor: Stewart S. Warren

fixedandfree.anthology@gmail.com

Cover photo and book design: Stewart S. Warren

Mercury HeartLink
www.heartlink.com

Contents

Acknowledgments

Publisher's Note

Introduction

Dedication

ARUN AHUJA
Monsoon Memory   *1*

TIMOTHY B. ANDERSON
Ode: Toulouse Lautrec (after *La Toilette*)   *2*

PRISCILLA BACA Y CANDELARIA
Democracy   *4*

CHANDRA BALES
Written of You   *6*

HAKIM BELLAMY
The Origin of the Hand Shake   *8*

SHIRLEY BALANCE BLACKWELL
Low-tide Catechism   *10*

SANDI BLANTON
Watching Little Daryl   *12*

JOANNE BODIN
Royal   *14*

BENJAMIN BORMANN
Shorn   *16*

JOE BOTTONE
And Then We're Drawn Away   *17*

RICH BOUCHER
Posing for My Master   *18*

KARIN BRADBERRY
Crazy Woman Creek   *21*

DEBBI BRODY
No Relation to Sartre- a goddess poem   *23*

GARY BROWER
The Armadilliad   *25*

BILLY BROWN
Roberta   *29*

LAUREN CAMP
Building   *30*

GREG CANDELA
Thanks John Ashbury   *31*

GARY STEWART CHORRÉ
Black Stockings   *32*

DEE COHEN
My Husband Rescues a Plant   *33*

CARLOS CONTRERAS
I Don't Know Much   *35*

DEBORAH COY
Six Fingered Man   39

SUSY CRANDALL
Sublime Sublimation   41

SYLVIA RAMOS CRUZ
A Surgical Memory   44

JULIE DUNLEAVY
Updike at the End   46

BILL EPLER
Opus 77 (Halloween)   47

MARY FOGARTY
The Time Will Come   50

ELIZABETH ANN GALLIGAN
Holy Obligation   51

TERESA GALLION
Stretch has left the Playing Field   52

PATRICIA GILLIKIN
I Want to Cultivate a Stillness in Me   53

LAURA GREEN
Maenad Seeking Magus   55

KATRINA K. GURASCIO
Remembrance   56

KENNETH P. GURNEY
Becoming Impossible   57

ELENE GUSCH
At the "Rendezvous"   59

DALE HARRIS
Tryptich   60

BEATLICK PAMELA HIRST
The Coming Solitude   61

REV. REBECCA GUILE HUDSON
Depressed With Halo   64

ANTHONY HUNT
Arising In Albuquerque   65

LISA JACOBS
Klezmerquerque 2011   66

ARDITH JOHNSON
Beside the Highway   68

KATHAMANN
Beyond A Reasonable Doubt   69

ZACHARY KLUCKMAN
Scrapbook for the Lonely   71

SARI KROSINSKY
Odysseus' abandoned crewman discusses Cyclops etiquette   73

WAYNE LEE
Carrizozo Waitress   75

MARIETTA LEIS
Blue   76

CAROL LEWIS
    Walking to Work   *78*

MARIA LEYBA
    Collecting Names   *79*

GINA MARSELLE
    hand-me-down   *81*

MIRANDA MARSELLE
    Night Sky   *82*

MARY MCGINNIS
    Black Wind   *83*

DON MCIVER
    The Awning   *84*

MERIMÉE MOFFITT
    Nativity   *86*

SAMUEL MOORMAN
    Geography for Dummies   *87*

YASMEEN NAJMI
    Gulf Ghazal   *88*

CAROL MOSCRIP
    Shadows   *90*

BILL NEVINS
    Bad News, a Waltz   *93*

BRUCE NOLL
    In Place   *97*

MARY OERTEL-KIRSCHNER
  Rue Jacob   *98*

JILL A. OGLESBY
  Geimhreadh *99*

MARILYN O'LEARY
  Drought *101*

KATE PADILLA
  New Mexico Heirloom *102*

SCOTT PALMER
  Bukowski Suicide *103*

ANNMARIE H. PEARSON
  Sister Josephine *106*

CHARLES POWELL
  Begging Eyes *108*

ROBERT REEVES
  Here Be Dragons *111*

ELIZABETH ROLL
  The Quarter *112*

BONNIE RUCOBO
  My Mother's Brother *115*

GEORGIA SANTA MARIA
  Ojito Arroyo (for Mary) *117*

DANIEL SCHWARTZ
  Necropolis *119*

ELAINE SCHWARTZ
    Paseo en El Paso, 1945   121

LAUREN SCHWARTZ
    Acropolis   123

BEATLICK JOE SPEER
    Glad to Be   125

MARILYN STABLEIN
    Curing the Bones   128

K. K. (KITTY) TODOROVICH
    At Auntie's Viewing   130

SAL TREPPIEDI
    One Moment Past Midnight   132

AARON TRUMM
    Walking Dead   133

BOB WARREN
    Sonny   137

STEWART S. WARREN
    The Writing Class   140

RICHARD WOLFSON
    Broken Time   142

JASON YURCIC
    Winter in the Desert   143

    Contributors

Acknowledgments

Albuquerque poets Sandi Blanton, Billy Brown, Kenneth Gurney, Zachary Kluckman and Merimée Moffitt were there at the beginning. The monthly Fixed and Free poetry readings grew out of their 2008 meeting.

Special thanks to Sam Peifer, owner of the Fixed & Free Bike Shop[1], who generously provided space, at no charge, for our earliest readings. Sam also welcomed the use of his business name for our reading series and this anthology. How delightful that types of bicycles[2] are types of poetry[3]!

Chery Klairwator of The Source for Creating Sacredness[4] has provided beautiful homes for our readings in their Garden room, Blue room and outdoor deck at a generous rate since 2009.

Merimée Moffitt was especially helpful during the first three years of Fixed and Free, hosting readings and holding several at her home.

Kenneth Gurney also enthusiastically hosted.

The editorial team members were indispensible. Billy Brown conceived this anthology. Elaine Schwartz pushed it beyond the conceptual stage. Elaine and Greg Candela served as able and dedicated referees for submissions. Stewart Warren of Mercury HeartLink[5] designed the cover and layout and steered the team through the complexities of online, on-demand publishing.

This anthology is, in itself, an acknowledgment of all the poets who participate in the Fixed and Free poetry community. Thanks to all of them for their inspiring poetry and their assistance at the readings, including their financial contributions.

1.   From the Fixed & Free Bike Shop web site: "Albuquerque's premier source for fixed gear and single speed bikes, components, and culture." www.fixedandfree.com

2.   From Wikipedia: "A **fixed-gear** bicycle (or **fixed-wheel** bicycle, sometimes known as a **fixie**) is a bicycle that has no free wheel, meaning it cannot coast, as the pedals are always in motion when the bicycle is moving."

3.   From Wikipedia: "**Fixed verse** forms are a kind of template or formula that poetry can be composed in. The converse of fixed verse is **Free verse** poetry, which by design has little or no pre-established guidelines." The Haiku, Sestina and Sonnet are examples of fixed verse forms.

4.   From The Source's web site: "We are a diverse bodywork and wellness center, as well as a gathering place that hosts classes, art shows, performances, and celebrations." www.thesourceabq.com

5.   From Mercury HeartLink's web site: "Mercury HeartLink works closely with writers and other artists to offer solutions that are client-centered and provide support in the larger realm of self-realization." www.heartlink.com

Publisher's Note

Established in 1994, Mercury HeartLink evolved from HeartLink Integration Therapy, a family systems counseling practice and healing events enterprise. At that time activities were expanded to include Internet based projects and printing solutions that foster humanistic values and creative access to information.

As an alternative to large commercial publishing houses and the unguided and less professional endeavors of self-publishing, Mercury HeartLink works closely with writers and other artists to offer solutions that are client-centered and provide support in the larger realm of self-realization.

Mercury HeartLink welcomes individual and collaborative works of educational, cultural and community value. These may include creative non-fiction, memoir and poetry, but all have two things in common: an authenticity on the part of the author and a responsibility to positive social impact.

It was with pleasure then that Mercury HeartLink accepted the opportunity to collaborate with Fixed and Free Poetry anthology editors on this project, an endeavor that lifts people up and joins them in a community of artistic expression.

Stewart S. Warren, Albuquerque 2011

Introduction

How does someone who hated poetry for over thirty years end up writing an introduction to a poetry anthology?

Mr. Austin was teaching a unit on poetry in eleventh grade English. He read a sweet poem, perhaps by Robert Frost, about a small bird flitting from tree to tree in the forest. To add sound effects from my seat in the back row, I whistled a few gentle trills. I thought I was hidden behind a large football player and would not get caught.

Of course I *was* caught and kicked out of class for three days! No big deal, except that Mr. Austin ordered me to move my desk into the hall outside his classroom. As students went in and out of the classroom I was jabbed in the chest, clunked on the head or otherwise ridiculed, adding to my punishment. I emerged from this humiliating experience with an intense dislike for poetry.

For the next 35 years I had no interest in poetry. I never read it or wrote it. I ignored poetry assignments in my college Western Civilization courses. Poetry was not going to play a part in my life.

A few weeks after my 18-year-old daughter Elizabeth was killed in a single car accident in 1996, I stood in tears at my mother's grave in Michigan and scribbled on a napkin my very first poem, a grief poem entitled "Between Brown Bookends." I compared my daughter's and my mother's dark brown hair and eyes, their dimples, and how their deaths affected me. I recalled sweet memories of cuddling on the couch, with my mother as a young boy and with my little girl.

I was amazed at the intensity of my feelings, and I was astonished by the enormous relief produced by this outpouring of words. In a matter of 30 minutes, my distaste for poetry was suddenly transformed into a deep gratitude for poetry's powerful possibilities. For several years

I continued to write grief poems and share them with other bereaved parents, which proved therapeutic for me and for many dozens of them. I came to value poetry deeply as a means of expressing and sharing powerful feelings. After my own grief had subsided, my poetry was inspired by art, music, nature, romantic love and admiration for many wonderful individuals in my life.

As I moved my poetry into a wider public arena the monthly <u>Central Avenue</u> poetry reading became my principal poetry home. I published a few poems in local publications, including <u>Central Avenue</u>, and in April 2005 Sandi Blanton and I began hosting Quarterly Poetry Open Houses in our living room, to provide a more informal venue for poets.

When the <u>Central Avenue</u> readings and publication ended in 2007, I searched for a new poetry home. I simply could not tolerate the vacuum left by the end of <u>Central Avenue</u>, and so I began to plan a new monthly poetry reading.

Since poetic expression is so important to me, I felt that other poets would also welcome a new regular poetry event. Our Fixed and Free poetry readings, which began in 2008, are the result of this belief. The name "Fixed and Free" comes from the bike shop in Albuquerque's Nob Hill which hosted our readings for the first several months, and I thank them for supporting us.

It is difficult to describe how inspired I am by every Fixed and Free reading. After hosting all but three of our nearly forty monthly readings, it sometimes seems exhausting, and I might say "I don't want to go tonight!" But I always do go and am always touched by the powerful self-expression coming from every one of our poets! Always, always, always I return home from Fixed and Free readings excited and energized to continue.

It is especially gratifying when poets new to Fixed and Free read for the first time. I feel like a father encouraging all my poetic "children" (of all ages) to bud and blossom. For each poet and for each poem she reads,

I sense the importance of her expression—laugh-out-loud humor, a precious family memory, a painful experience, a political passion, a reflection of something beautiful—feelings of joy, fear, anger, love, warmth.

I am proud of the variety and excellence of all our featured poets. It is a wonderfully intimate experience to hear wider and deeper samples of each poet's expression. We receive precious glimpses of their entire lives, which is otherwise difficult in our hurried and harried culture.

When we broadcast our call for submissions for this anthology, we restricted eligibility to those poets who had read at Fixed and Free by the end of the submission period, or were scheduled to be a featured reader by the end of 2011. Many poets who had not yet read at Fixed and Free quickly arranged to do so in order to qualify for inclusion in this anthology! The last two readings before the end of the submission period lasted well beyond our usual end time.

I am astounded by the quality of the poems herein. As I read through the entire collection, I am moved by poem, after poem, after poem, a powerful affirmation of my transformation from poetry hater to poetry lover!

I am grateful to all the poets who have read at Fixed and Free. My life is enriched by your poetry. I trust that this collection honors you, represents your talents to the wider poetry world and strengthens our Fixed and Free community.

Billy Brown, Albuquerque, 2011

For poets on the page and on the stage
who contribute to the Fixed and Free community

To truth and beauty
from which poetry springs

Arun Ahuja

Monsoon Memory

When the rain gods were done
with their hail-o-*rama* run
The *koyal* wailed its all-clear call
The roadside gutters beckoned all
us frog hunters to a fresh attack
charging to the rhythm of the squeaky smack
of rubber *chuppals* flicking at calloused heels
and slushy whining mudguards on bicycle wheels

to where
Paper boats meandered on the water (puddled)
by the banyan tree where the orphan huddled
crushing hailstones between his chattering teeth
while the scent of *halava* swayed to *Natya Sangeet* (*)   ༁

* Sanskrit for Dance Music for a formal, high society temple dance.

TIMOTHY B. ANDERSON

Ode: Toulouse Lautrec (after *La Toilette*)

"Only once," you said. "I will pose for you,
only once, and no one must know.
I will tie my hair in a chignon, and
I will turn my back to you,
with my face lowered, away from prying eyes.

"You will not see me without a dress,
or from the front to expose my treasures;
the chemise will be lowered to my waist,
and a spread will cover the floor, under my
stockings I will not toss over the chair.

"You will paint my hair the color
of fire, and straighten the curls,
to keep prying eyes and minds away
from the face, the chin... me.

"You will paint me here, where I sit,
in my toilette, but a different
scene will be painted,
one in which your studio
is forefront and foremost." she insisted.

I would have painted her anywhere,
be it farm or factory, studio or salon;
for her beauty was beyond compare,

her hair silky and soft, falling in cascades
past a shoulder the color of porcelain.

Only that once have I posed her,
but I have painted her a thousand times
with each stroke of the brush,
each curve of the crayon,
and with each movement of my hand.   ϡ

PRISCILLA BACA Y CANDELARIA

Democracy

A dictator's thirty year reign
coming to an end
Hollywood greedily asking
what will this *cost*
when we need an Egyptian set backdrop?
Cha-ching!
Oil companies crying foul,
now that ports, refineries, people
shall not be exploited.
Cha-ching!
While thousands upon thousands
pour in from across the Nile delta
no longer able to live
on $2 dollars a day wages
While the wealthy
pilfer wealth
to Swiss accounts
Cha-ching!
Governments struggling
with the fall
of a bought and
paid for regime
A region so
wealthy engulfed
in poverty
Excessive wealth
Despicable poverty

Cha-ching Democracy
at its best
Leaving its people . . .
Cha-ching-gados!   ҩ

CHANDRA BALES

Written of You

White light startles sheltered eyes, invites me to think with you.
On star-borne snows and softened haze I step in sync with you.

We wander still rooms, promenade wide halls through hollow breath;
I hold your platinum head, lightly trace the link with you.

On Devon cream our journey floats, on hearths and on rivers.
We bite into mince tarts and tea. And I sink with you.

Evening clouds haunt my landscape in their perfection,
drape their seamless water curves with the pink of you.

Around glass shoulders garden faeries weave yellow castles,
wrap their chants against stored floods; they stand at the brink with you.

I heard a jest but yesterday of sisters and your country,
doubtful and bemused, until I shared a wink with you.

All of England's hills and towns burned dry and brittle raw,
remaining coals ignorant of the need to drink of you.

The empty fields once wept for the loss laid upon your palm.
Welled seas swallowed your joy and sealed their fractured chink with you.

Faster you run, and some memories must fade into green.
Stones fall behind pale shadows, now pearls in the blink of you.

Some nights I dream the circle of your touch, your voice.
Moon-glow whispers Chandra, warm in the ink of you.   ❧

HAKIM BELLAMY

The Origin of the Hand Shake

"It's thought to imply that 'one holds no weapon...'"
As the teacher trails off into teary-eyed diatribes of broken customs
Breaking promises and fractured people
Hands don't always help

And they're learning to do for self
In the generation of "Get ya hands up!" instead of getting hand-outs
It wasn't rap nor robbery when the Puritans John Wayne played
     made 'em reach for the sky
No sticking up for our children
When high school seniors, ours from Head Start
Who've been sprinting past standards in two languages,
Don't have enough Apple Pie in their parents to reach this
American
Dream
Act.
It's when the lines lose character and our rap ain't keepin' it real
The constitution becomes a sit-com script cause we're too old to
     believe in fairy-tales
Our tired, our poor and our weak might as well be falling asleep in
     your drama class
Cause it's all about class drama and
They won't matriculate brown-ass-hands that might not have the right
     answer
But CERTAINLY have another narrative.

And now the classroom is

Full of so many dark raised hands they want to call it domestic
    violence
Domestic terrorism once each and every student's raised right hand
Folds five fingers until there's a fist inside of it.

These are the benchmarks of behavior we need to publicize and not
    privatize
But all we get are stories about how our children are failing
Since they are only fifty percent proficient at reading, reciting, essay
    writing and multiplying our lies

Knowing our history and their present
An open hand
Means nothing
To a child
Who is much more concerned with whether that hand is held or
    shaking

Cause when she's only four
And this hand shake... is what's left from her "night before"
There are lots of answers
But only one question...
Why?   ✎

SHIRLEY BALANCE BLACKWELL

Low-tide Catechism

The hour for Nature's confessional is low tide,
in which all is revealed, from barnacled docks
to oyster beds left desolate by the sea's retreat.
When waters ebb, secrets yield, as if a shield had dropped
between priest and penitent, with no room to hide.

In this pulse, shore birds with blurring scissors' stride
and eyes like sharp, black beads swarm the flats; perform
an inquisition of the shallows; their greedy beaks
roll shells aside, probe gravel shifted by the tide
in search of small, reluctant martyrs fleeing home.

Crustaceans burrow in contrition, pretend
to disappear, like secrets cloistered in the mind.
Do they hear the slide of shifting grains with dread,
or fear the shovel bill that seines the drifting sands
set tumbling by the piper's hungry tread?

The burnished stems of wetlands rushes,
blessed by the holy waters' inland flow
and touched by slanting sunlight, come aglow,
as if a master's hand were wielding them, like brushes,
painting domes of air in tints of Michelangelo.

When tides recede, the marshes wear a coat of mud;
reeds fade, as if the artist branded his meek tools
heretics and abandoned them, arrayed upon a rack.

Then, they put on sackcloth hues, stand in dull,
mute rows, like monks exploring silence to find God.

But why should I presume that low tide has revealed
a world where the ordained is reason to repent?
Although I recoil, nature seems at ease in *dishabille*;
untidiness provokes no shame, seems no less Heaven sent
than flood. Rising, falling: an equal sacrament. ❧

SANDI BLANTON

Watching Little Daryl

I'm watching Little Daryl,
a tiny black and white kitten
sleeping on his back
with his paws over his head.
He is slowly sliding down
behind the red sofa cushion,
but he doesn't know that.
He is completely relaxed
gone to some place
of blissful surrender.
I stare at his small soft body
in its furry tuxedo
pulsing with the peace
that passes understanding.

An amazing miracle
this minute mass of fur and bone
with all the necessary parts
put together just so
to make a kitten,
every molecule precisely connected
to every other molecule
lined up perfectly to form
tiny ears and paws,
miniature eyes and nose.
And all the little internal organs
doing their little jobs perfectly

while he sleeps oblivious
with his arms stretched over his head.

He is dreaming,
riding on the breath,
miraculous prana
lifting and falling
like gentle ocean waves
carrying him deeper and
deeper into nirvana.
I breathe with him
lifting, falling
pulsing, throbbing
in, out
up, down
searching
for my own heaven.   ℘

JOANNE BODIN

Royal

I am royal, Queen Mother
queen of palatial household
queen of three balanced meals a day
queen of five hours sleep a night
ruler supreme of providing a stimulating
environment for an active toddler and
a curious newborn
of driving the royal carriage
to the marketplace
of choosing the most natural
nutritious foods for their royal diet
and of remembering to buy only special
foods for His Majesty's low cholesterol diet
I am royal time keeper
queen of all the chores done before
His Royal Highness comes home
so it looks like the royal palace glistened
and glittered that way all day
in anticipation of his return
I am queen of runny noses and aspirin
and of fear
will the fever break tonight?
should we let our friend's brat visit
so soon after the weeks of illness and relapses?
I am Queen of the royal bed
between dreams and nightmares
embraces and blurry-eyed kisses

Queen of the royal hound
and his nightly escapades
I am royalty for sure
I am reminded every hour of every day
of my importance
my heroic pivot atop the throne of survival
yet you sneer when my gown wrinkles
or drags from misuse
you shrug at my small talk
of the day's events
you act surprised that my throne excludes you
so much of the time
what did you expect
a nightingale in a gilded cage?   ❧

BENJAMIN BORMANN

Shorn

I am a sweater on the
shoulders of an old woman.

She moves like fall
branches—every rasping
step calls the dead
down to be counted.

She is small and frail,
but has worked
lifetimes of men,
then buried them.
Her face is
their gravestone,
each wrinkle an epitaph,
each sad look a eulogy.

Eventually she will disrobe
me as well.
She promises
to be gentle, telling
me on that day her
eyes will smile.   ✑

JOE BOTTONE

And Then We're Drawn Away

Am I lost at sea or am I burning

Who can I ask in this sweet asylum of joyful craziness

Was that voice a night bird

Was what I saw real, another man's loneliness
        a rice cake, a stone?

A little grey fox comfortable in the daylight of our presence
trots towards the house now that we're gone
        'I can steal a bone or a rice cake'

And then other things happen
        and we're drawn away   ❧

RICH BOUCHER

Posing for My Master

Oh, hello, my dearest Government,
I am vigilant white shirt standing here
on the Dorothy wheat fields
of Elysian Revolutionaryness,
the ones with all the purple grain
in my office in this building of my house,
and I will but once speak my peace once,
and then my peace I will give to you.

I believe in the invincible price of freedom,
and also that the Statue of Liberty exists;
I believe in the fidgety P Diddy liturgy
of the American Thanksgiving word,
and in the power of search and seizure
and I, like you, too, pray that the Taliban
will always be the people who aren't me.
Therefore, TSA, if that is your real name,
before I take flight on your young, pretty airplane,
I willingly and humbly submit all of my body
to your special, laser-of-the-future photography
that gives me all the radiation my growing cells need,
in the very and same poignant way
that Dr. Bruce Banner was created.

Transportation Security Administration,
I only ask that you capture all of my beauty,
every moist, sun-kissed, aching, dewy inch,

every every of my only only in all of my look at this,
every silken, billowing-white-sheet covered place;
please, photograph me tenderly and slowly;
be sensitive, be the edge of a rose petal upon my nape;
be the "shhhhhhhhh" to my "hmmmm, what's that?";
let your eyes be like hands that kiss my music into silence;
take very clear, up-close and detailed photographs of me
in all my blessed, hard, angular and muscley perfection;
capture how like two bowls of kittenish soul my eyes can seem;
mark these hands and feet that type manifestos about
how the night is like a country road and vice versa,
all of my body's charming hills and hairs,
the evidence of manhood between my nipples and chest,
the fleshy rise and promontory of my sexual cock,
the mischievous navel between my center of gravity,
become aware of how I am a man
with all your brave and sophisticate cameras;
see and portray for all the world
every one of my form's gentle and breathtaking curves,
so like sand dunes of muscle and finger,
the cleavage of my rippling, oily pectorals
as they shake and flex where I stand
above the summertime sprinkler;
not shooting all of this malleable and compliant skin
means that the terrorists will have had epic win;
focus on my wistful and pensive buttocks,
like two twin Volkswagens made of meat they are,
parked very close, so close to one another,
snap an artful shot, won't you please,
of every single hole that I have to offer,
my mouth, my ears, my outlet and escape hatch,
so like the open mouths of baby birds in a nest.

Make me your own,
and ask me in a whisper
how anyone could ever fly
without this.

I am ready to be the Leda
to your electronic Swan;
your aggression excites me so much
I will hand you my boarding pass with a smile.

And, oh, my beloved supervisors,
if you feel that you need more from me
than mere boudoir photography can give,
why then, please touch me in all of my places
until, hushed and sweaty, you are satisfied
that the truth is a secret safe in your hands;
take my please-be-gentle and be rough;
love me tough, give me the unbelievable pleasure,
give me the speaking-in-tongues in my throat;
use your lips and official mouth europeanly;
make me afraid of the dark once more
and get me all rigid; make me ready
to offer up my half of maybe a baby;
bring me to the verge of paradise
with the back of your gloved and dominant hand.

Anything you want me to do, I need to do,
whatever you want, whatever it takes
to help make this dangerous world a safer place to be.   ❧

KARIN BRADBERRY

Crazy Woman Creek

Wyoming sports a horse,
a bucking bronco so crazy
neither man nor woman
could tame its wildness bare-
handed. There were plenty of creeks,
but could you drink the water?

Everyone needed water:
Indians, white men, horses
alike. They named every creek
in the drought-stricken territory: Crazy,
Coyote, Pine, Buffalo, Middle Bear,
Elk, Lightning, Sage, Young Woman.

The legends about women
were never good: risking their lives to haul water,
attacked by settlers, Sioux and bear,
counted lucky if buried in Dead Horse.
If they didn't die, they went crazy
from grief, drowned themselves in creeks.

Wildcats prowled those creeks,
too fast for a heavy woman
to outrun, her panicked crazy
flight, skitter sloshing water
from clanging pails, her hoarse
cries useless, too much to bear.

When her time came, she learned to bear
down, hope for the familiar creak
of front step, whinny of husband's horse.
For every new mother, another woman
died, spared the chores of fetching water,
chopping wood, waiting to go crazy.

No doctor could help, no cure for crazy
weather, luck or fate. Just the bare
bones of survival: cold water
and sweet grass from Antelope Creek,
men who hunted with rifles or bows, women
who cooked, and always the horses.

But at last the water in the old creek dried up
leaving crazy cracked lines, trees that could not bear,
worn-out women and horses longing for green.   ❧

DEBBI BRODY

No Relation to Sartre- a goddess poem

The goddess of nothingness
flies in from nowhere
a killdeer winging her way
through a dream,

she blesses me,
ties a glittering ribbon
around my neck, knots
it in a heart shape
beneath my sternum.

She says, *empty your mind*
feel air whistle through,
find dark, light, shame,
shadow, brilliance.

She says, *empty your house,*
a wren does not take root
in any one tree. Use a sickle,
clear away excess. Chambers
should echo with rain.

> *Empty*
your mouth of lines left unsaid.
Put them under the slicing sword
until they fall into little letters
left on the floor. Fill your flowering

life with words of forgiveness
as you wend your way through
vacated hours. ❧

GARY BROWER

The Armadilliad

"The oldest known symbol of the universe is the circle. In ancient Egypt & Greece, ... the symbol of the snake eating its tail has been known as the *ourabouros*, signifying unity & eternity."
—D. Bessinger, *Living Ethics*.

I

Of more than twenty species,
marked with three to twelve bands,
all related to anteaters,
most common are nine-banded armadillos
who range from northern Mexico
to the American Southwest.

Unique in nature, they produce
four offspring from one egg,
no more, no less.

Only the three-banded version
can roll itself into a ball
for protection like
an armored *ourabouros*.

A throwback to primeval eras,
their coats like chain-mail armor
they might be perfect, standing upright in old castles,

holding spear or sword in claw-like hands;
or, the shell hollowed out for helmets.

If humans were smaller
or armadillos larger
we can imagine how
they might have changed history:
Hannibal crossing the Alps to attack Rome
with herds of armadillos
instead of war elephants.

Maharajahs of ancient India
with armies of attack-armadillos,
gondolas of soldiers on their backs,
driven by *mahouts,*
their natural armor
deflecting arrows of enemy archers.

Although, since they burrow
in the ground for safety,
fear could be a problem.

History changes in direct proportion
to your distance from the ground.

II

"Them armadillers yusta come
no further north than Texas,"
said the Okie from Okmulgee,
"now they's all the way up in Kansas,
seen'em all over the roads.

I think it's a sign uh the end uh the world,
like one uh them plagues before the Rapture,
but ya never know what them critters knows,
they might can talk to God."

"Maybe," he said spitting tobacco juice
like a grasshopper, "they's the meek what
will inherit the earth, when cars and trucks
have no fuel."

Straddling armadillo carcasses
along Oklahoma highways,
scattering crows and coyotes,
I thought he might have a point.

Armadillos, with no
original peccadilloes,
navigate by instinct on the ground,
by faith through the earth,
quadreplicate endlessly,
leave martyrs in the roadway arena
to motorized jaguars,
and wait, without knowing,
for the Coming of Chuy* Armadillo
as he unrolls the trinity of his three body-bands,
Father, Son and Holy Anteater,
from the circle of himself,
proclaiming, like Heraclitus,
"One unifies all,"
promising the Armadilliad
it will never burrow out of fear again,
announcing they shall rule

with their long, sticky tongues,
just like us,
but without the lies. ✌

*Chuy = A nickname for those named "Jesus" in Mexico.

BILLY BROWN

Roberta

to see you again
after three weeks
is like seeing a daughter
gone fourteen years

her tan skin
her long brown hair
her dark brown eyes
her long delicate fingers
dancing on violin strings
her small nose
her smiling lips
gently pressed together in effort
are all yours now
 in blessed reincarnation

her flesh, her moisture,
her ashes, her steam,
her grace, her beauty
miraculously reassembled

a divine gift   ❧

LAUREN CAMP

Building

Like one hand, the brothers
            hammer and drill. Like one eye,
                    they turn blue lines to beams,
                    inches to interiors.
            Like one mind, they create
            the door
            to the future.   ❧

GREG CANDELA

Thanks John Ashbury

Sleep, like skin, is porous
with dreams that leak
up and down and between
stones in the well of gravity.

Sometimes, if we wake, sodden
we remember to pull the string
light. We cannot figure what is in
the basement being worked on.

It's just a guess because this
is the place we descend to
on narrow cellar stairs down
the top three steps on tiptoes.

All the talk in daylight
won't change that.   ❧

GARY STEWART CHORRÉ

Black Stockings

Long legs, black stockings and a creviced face.
Old before her time,
    walking the boardwalk,
        working for that dime.
But who is she going to call, anyway?
There was a time when ..., doesn't matter now.
Musn't get a run in the black stockings.
Once you start, you cannot quit the race.
She can never finish first
but must be sure not to finish last;
the price is too high.
At one time she sang songs of hope and joy.
That was before her wings were broken,
forgot all those songs, doesn't matter now.
Old before her time,
    walking the boardwalk,
        working for that dime.
Where did the child go?
What happened to the smile?
Lost in the canals,
    red as Mars,
        that scar the face of shame. ❧

DEE COHEN

My Husband Rescues a Plant

Oh crap, the thing is practically dead:
stunted branches hollowed out
and hardly a brown leaf left.
I haven't watered it in months,
not since November
when I shoved it onto the patio
between the rusty grill and the busted table,
and abandoned it,
tipped against the wrought iron rails,
for winter to take a swing at,
do some real damage.
Then next spring, I'd drag it out
by the cuff of the pot,
wrap my hands around
its thin throated branches,
fling it in the dumpster, and listen
to the satisfying sound
of dry dirt hitting bottom.

But it's too late.
I watch him through the kitchen window.
He holds a plastic pitcher brimmed with water.
His lower lip is pushed out,
eyebrows locked with worry,
as he administers small sips
onto the parched soil.
How tenderly he moves his hands

over the limp body,
his fingers feeling the bark,
a blind search for buds of growth.
And now, he pushes his face
right into the last of the blighted leaves,
and I know, *I just know*,
he's murmuring something sweet.   ❧

CARLOS CONTRERAS

I Don't Know Much

I don't know much but I know this much is true
Babies are born innocent
ruined nearly immediately
and sometimes ignored completely

I don't know much but I know this much is true
Pens are sometimes as sharp as needles
and sometimes I can't stop myself despite them…
I am victim to the madness and the mayhem

However I know this much is true,
That sometime in my life I will find and lose love
forget about it along the edges of a bottle and
remember it when it goes empty

I know that the ends of cigarettes burn
like the fires inside us
until we are all nothing but ash
This world will be more than dust

I don't know much
But I do know you hear me now
Nothing in life is guaranteed
but death
Cold can sometimes feel hot
and vice versa
We may fall victims to our vices but

embrace them for lack of better entertainment

I don't know much but I do know this
Somewhere right now, a child is laughing
jaw unhinged at the possibility of forgetting
Lips hanging on the possibility of laughter again
tomorrow

I don't know much but I know this much is true
Birds don't just sing to hear themselves,
they sing so that you may want to get out of bed in the morning
and tell them to shut the fuck up

I do know that
my television hates me
It calls me fat without saying so
Tells me I am blind to the world unless
it shows me something it likes
and wants me to buy
I am broke

tired and hungry
But I know this much is true,
so are you
Or headed in that direction,
If you need a way there I'll help you
Look at the bottom of your pockets
If lint is all you find
perfect

I don't know much but I know this much is true
If I didn't write I'd die

wither up and fade away...
like new growth in the sun...

I know the sun sets, in the east
and rises in the west
I know that I love you like the sun

I don't know much but I know this
The most important things in this world fit through the eye
of a needle, because they aren't things at all
I know that I can stick this life out with the promise of a better one
on the other side
Find me there.

I've lost myself
in the noise of my heart beat
in the madness between my ears
I know you don't hear me intently
but hear me here...

Here,
is the beginning of now and then
of the future and the forever of what we plan
to create
I don't know much except that
smiles or lack thereof
tell the whole truth
We're skeletons playing guessing
games
crossing bones and blowing wishes
in the wind,
because we are worth no more than dirt...

I don't know much,
But I know this much is true...
Humans are defined by the laugh lines
and calluses,
bruises
and scars,
markings of memory
so like jumping in a pool and sinking
I want you to remember me.
I don't know much but I know this much is true
Tomorrow
I will remember
today.   ❧

DEBORAH COY

Six Fingered Man

It was funny
how we met.
It was on a bus
and there was
standing room only.
It lurched
and I had
to remove my hand
from my pocket
to catch myself.
I was forced to
expose my six fingers.
My extra digit
lay useless and flaccid
above my third knuckle,
my second bird,

but she noticed
and followed me home.
A few days later
she showed up at my door
holding a small velvet box.
It was a ring perfect to fit
that dangling dialer.

When we go out
she never allows me

to wear gloves
but insists we dance
with my hand resting
spiderlike
on her shoulder.

I have been worried lately;
she has been teaching
the man with two tongues
how to speak
another language.   ❧

SUSY CRANDALL

Sublime Sublimation

Financial insecurity
my paycheck held hostage
to missing paperwork
could have me hopping mad

A spark to ignite
a change in my work life
a conflagration, despite this
uncomfortably muggy weather.

Aggravated by the demands of
other people, it's
my karma to get hit up
by needy people.

Flashpoint? Or should I beat
a hasty retreat?
Some might see it as a mean retreat
but I don't care.

It's time for me to surrender
to my divine inception as, as…
a Porn Star!
But not just any porn star
not like those dead-eyed girls
hiding behind masks of
high-gloss paint

shame-bound and full of hate
for the automatons they service

I'll be like that one girl I saw
(only one out of so many!)
in that tiny photo
in the back of the AVN catalog
I looked into so many faces to find her
I know some of you know
what I'm talkin' about.

I'll be weightless
winging my way from
stamen to pistil
dancing between the flowers
drawing the nectar

in pure joy
like a butterfly or hummingbird
choosing my co-stars
for the sunsprays of laugh lines radiating out
from the margins of their kind eyes

For their hungry reciprocity and
ability to nibble and munch
the crimson up through
the skin of my cheeks and
nether petals.

My nether petals...
transforming them from a pale translucent pink
to a tropical flush so distracting

that spirits pause in their
ghostly ascension to
admire their radiance... ❧

SYLVIA RAMOS CRUZ

A Surgical Memory

Breeze rustles your hair,
fans out the threading gray like
fingers riffling pages in a book.

We sit under dazzling autumn sun,
sip Japanese tea from glazed clay cups
that remind you of traveling home
on Indian Railways, uncured clay shards
stained with Darjeeling scattered along the tracks—
cups used once and tossed not to mark
the way home but to ensure a safe return.

I remember the night we spent under the OR lamps
your gloved hands showering reflected light
like New Year sparklers—clamping, cutting, tying,
casting shattered liver into buckets—
reclaiming a man's life.

You left me to close the belly.
I loved being part of the rescue.
I resented you for going to sleep while I toiled
'til dawn to keep your masterpiece alive.

We were bonded, you and I, in that
thin struggle between life and death;
urgency infusing our anatomy.

We touch briefly on family, work, play.
You golf almost every day. I sometimes write poetry.
A flick of your slender wrist still punctuates your words.
I look at your eyes and feel no tremor;
gaze into green depths and see no leaves.

I remember why I loved you.
Yes, your tight cinnamon body
and, oh, your flying hands. ❧

JULIE DUNLEAVY

Updike at the End

John, without wanting to go,
knew he was going to the next world quick
in the way a Virginia Creeper drops
with the slightest pull
and lets go of the wall.

While I, in my life-long denial, seize
every opportunity for resistance,
cling like a tree to the sky, inch my roots
out another breath into the earth
as if to hold me firm on the planet.
My resistance is fierce as if in battle
down and climbing back, a holding on
to defeat death.

All illusion Freud would say,
the war lost from the beginning.

But not for John. He didn't
mention war or think Thanatos
the victor. He thought of resurrection,
the undefended oak bare for the return
of the vine, and like the Virginia
Creeper, he let go with grace.

What muscle is that?   ❧

BILL EPLER

Opus 77 (Halloween)

Halloween
for the boy in a small town
was quite an event
with paper sacks
loaded to the top
with popcorn balls, Hershey bars, and hard candy for
winters in Alaska.
the costume making
started after school
and often went on for an hour or two
under the auspices
of mostly older siblings and mothers
while the dusk of an evening evolved into
darkness between street lamps
unknown to city children.
gnomes of the night
giggling and sweaty
crisscrossed neighborhoods
on the other side of town
and breathlessly exchanged information
with devils, ghosts, and
masked faces
sometimes identical to your own,
about the bulb lit porches down the street.
here was your chance of the year
to stop being a kid or a student

and most of all
a life form without parents.

behind the garish mask
with its soggy breathing hole
held to your face
by a thin elastic band
was the you known only to yourself.
a breather of darkness,
the middle of the night you
with the radio by your bed turned on
singing secretly
to the massacred privacy of childhood.
occasionally the boy
would get out of bed
walk to the window
and breathe the secret winds of the night
while listening to the heartbeat of the town.
the daylight world awaiting him
now at bay
would skewer him in due course,
but for now, by the window, in the darkness
was freedom and romance.
with the radio in the background
whispering to him about worlds beyond
schools and churches
and families which claim to be finalities
the boy would cease to exist
utterly,
but not finally,
as a creature with three names
in a solar system family.

the boy embraced the darkness
like a lover
like a lover.
the boy embraced the darkness
like a lover.   ❧

MARY FOGARTY

The Time Will Come

The time will come when
young men with arms torn
and legs ripped off will return home
and ask for great sorrows to end.

The time will come when the
sobs of youth in battle
will teach there is no prosthetic
for the soul.

The time will come when we will
ride invisible winds of change
and in this time bond
with the stars.

Come! Come whoever you are.
Wanderer, worshipper,
lover of leaving,
yours is not a caravan of deceiving.

Even if you break vows a thousand times—
your time will come again and again.
For what you seek is seeking you.   ഔ

ELIZABETH ANN GALLIGAN

Holy Obligation

Today, I could not stay away.
The mountains declared I come
in a voice which rumbled down arroyos.
Errands and plans on hold,
I shifted priorities,
drove to the nearest trailhead.
A few red vines, yellow chamisa
saluted the season's shift.
On higher slopes, skeletal
aspen no longer quaked.
I gazed at my mountains' muted colors,
followed the flow of grey-beige shadows
sinuously crossing dun foothills,
felt the hairs rise on my arms
in the snappy autumn breeze.
Dark green piñons held out cones
sprung into caramel stars.
Underneath, plump juncos scratched.
I leaned down, kissed two fingers,
pressed them on cool granite,
felt its pulse, touched heart stone.
Mountains, like parents,
demand periodic pledges
of filial allegiance
and bless us when we come.   ❧

Teresa Gallion

Stretch has left the Playing Field

I think of age 35
and 135 pounds,
softball, volleyball,
tennis and bicycling,
walking pleasure miles.

I think of Stretch,
my softball name
as I do a split,
toe holding first base
ball in glove, umpire shouts,
You're out.

With a swan's grace
I rise, articulate
a fluid throw to second,
umpire shouts, You're out.
A double play and team
howls, Go Stretch.

Now at age 60,
190 pounds,
a split, a call to 9-1-1,
paramedics rake me off the ground.
Stretch has left the playing field.

PATRICIA GILLIKIN

I Want to Cultivate a Stillness in Me

I want to cultivate a stillness in me
a permission to be
a loose and easy feeling that I don't have to do that thing
that thing
that is always the next thing I have to do to make right
to fix
to wrap
in the thin sharp wire (of my soul)
to lift up with aching shoulders
not aching fingers and hands but shoulders alone
it's like this recurring dream I have:

I'm driving, but I'm in the back seat, I can't reach the wheel
can't get to the gas and the break and the clutch
and yet I drive
the car goes
And there's this panic in me
(in my soul)
that the car
won't go where it should

I want to find a soft grassy piece of ground inside me (in my soul)
it doesn't have to be fancy mowed planted human grass
it can be wild river grass,
bent over by the wind and the mild
flooding from the last monsoon storm
I want to sit (in my soul) on this spot and watch the light on the water

the movements of the sky the way the clouds embrace each other
the way the subtle ominous intricate closings and openings
glowing blue more light blue than I've ever seen
melts through
pierces the whiteness in unearthly patterns

I want to lose the sense that I have to fix things
I want to lose it in a dark alley somewhere
let it be kidnapped by nefarious beings and end up on a pirate ship
being retrained with new pirate skills
that would be good for it

I want to lose the sense that I have to keep on
that I'm not done
that it's not ever right
that I'm not ever finished with this poem
that I have to keep at it, keep at it
but mostly, I want to lose that drive, that inner push
because of the steady metal pain in my shoulder (in my soul)
I want to do
and let go
and let it be enough
I want to be satisfied with smaller pieces, with less,
let that be the new discipline that teaches me my craft
I want to let go this poem
so I will   ❧

LAURA GREEN

Maenad Seeking Magus

Frenzied female
I run these dark woods
search you out
in your hidden places
eluding capture
by Satyr's evil intent
I spurn the voice of Eros
polyphallic inducements
of Dionysian debauchery
do not lure me
I am no hetaera
nor foolish young nymph
deluded by Adonis' charm
Pannic flutes
do not soothe my soul
seeking only your magic
a lonely sentinel
in stoic stubbornness
I wait for you

KATRINA K. GURASCIO

Remembrance

We are not strangers.
This musk of rotting page and after shave,

I know this.

I could trace on a blank canvas,
with well trained fingers,
the curve of hair against cheekbones.

These grooves and gutters
are not unfamiliar.
They are a part of the past,
a part of every bit of who we are.

I know your skin
like the lines in my own reflection.
I know your eyes
like the freckles on my palm.

Duality lingers
in our sway,
in our remembrance.

We are not strangers.   ❧

KENNETH P. GURNEY

Becoming Impossible

I wish it had something to do with reason,
with a degree of difficulty,
but no, it started with my
walk on water trick.

Not that I meant to copy one of the Christ's
most cited miracles, but
I thought it a good compromise start
for my real goal of walking on air.

Also, I learned to bend light around my body
so your eye never receives my image. Really,
it was as easy as learning
the mariner's manual of knots.

There is the part of willing my molecules to change
so that wings sprouted from under my shoulder blades,
but that was a mostly-failure which spawned my desire
to be invisible due to the feathery patches on my back.

I thought if I can't fly I have enough time to walk
and some article I read about quantum mechanics,
or maybe a Heinlein book, gave me the idea
of walking on air.

It has something to do with my Roadrunner mentality
and the successful assertion of ignorance

in the meaningful accomplishment of what might,
otherwise, be considered impossible.

My true goal is to visit heaven before death
and make sure there is plenty to go around
of all the promised riches of the afterlife

before I join any one religion over another.   ❧

ELENE GUSCH

At the "Rendezvous"

Dried-up flies lie
on outspread wings,
little feet folded in repose,
on a white-painted ledge
beneath a wide window
emblazoned "Suisse Bakery"
A maroon painted stripe
hides the carnage
from public view
Their still-live cousins, curious,
briefly lap at the corpses
and return to buzzing
at the window
two feet from an open door
where more flies pour in
but none fly out
They cannot see
the big picture   ❧

DALE HARRIS

Tryptich

i

The Wolf Moon, moving
lonesome on the western sky,
hopes for snow tonight.

We run along the mesa,
follow in his bright, high tracks.

ii

Full moon in Scorpio,
such beauty! stay indoors
away from open windows.

Stars stagger home at dawn
drunk with lilac on their breath.

iii

When Persephone left home
her mother packed her a lunch,
"No good food where you're going,"
    Demeter said,

but the love-struck girl forgot,
ate a pomegranate instead.   ✎

BEATLICK PAMELA HIRST

The Coming Solitude

He is a poet I greatly admire
his heart is on his sleeve when he recites.
Recently, in a sad reflective moment,
he lamented,
"Everyone I love is going to die."

This is our common denominator—
our coming solitude.
We come here from an
ill-defined place to a sensory earth
a world of taste, touch, hearing,
smell and sight. We come all alone
and we will return to that place
again, alone, all alone.

My day of solitude has come
I no longer can taste Joe's lips
smell the nape of his neck
hear his melodious voice
touch him, see him.

It is frightening to see my known reality
splinter away one entity at a time:
first the neighborhood
parents, best friends
then the wars
and the economy

and now I have lost Joe.
The moorings of my knowledge
are so fallible
that I know nothing.

Except this:
I have had the privilege
of an exquisite and abiding love
my crutch and my strength.
And, Joe, your love lifted me up
gave me a status
I couldn't achieve on my own
and I will glorify your love
as I go forward without you.
I go without bitterness or anger.

As I progress into my solitary soul
my splintered soul,
for indeed we were one spirit,
I will pour out everything good
that we had together
into that void of pain
that this world has become.

I am called upon to be braver than ever before
to journey farther than ever before
give more generously than ever before
and help make this world a better place
for those who struggle and suffer.

I will do this in your name, Joe,
and carry forward the perfect love you gave me.

When I am emptied out, wrung out
I will pass beyond this coming solitude
into a new alternate reality.
I will love not resent
give not take
in your honor.   ❧

REV. REBECCA GUILE HUDSON

Depressed With Halo

He wears his depression,
scavenged at some
yard sale, bought
and sold on the cheap.

His pants hang
dejected, sad
drooping and dragging
two sizes too large.

His shoulders drip
with no self-confidence
have given up
bent, stooped and cringing.

His head hangs forward
on a spineless neck
crimped slightly sideways
to avoid long ago.

And a dark halo
shadows his every move
a weightless burden
imbued with persistent gravity.   ❧

ANTHONY HUNT

Arising In Albuquerque

Reassuring,

the sounds

crows outside
in the cold bare trees

the hum of the furnace below

the house creaks

eyes pried open
dark floaters drift every which way ...
on the white ceiling

oh . . . the warmth of our bodies

the glow.

Good . . .

oh . . . yet another . . .

"Good . . . Morning."

We are

still here.   ஒ

LISA JACOBS

Klezmerquerque 2011

I reach hands and eyes over the mesa
set two candlesticks on its desert table
we say a prickly pear ha motzi
and settle down to eat stir fry
with cholla chopsticks
Beth plays my ancestors on the fiddle
Margot reaches for home
anywhere
the strains of her clarinet rise
over hurdles
of 21st century
diaspora

Yosl twists yucca strands into swirling tzitzit
lifts diedle dee
joy from earth to sky
I resist the remembrance of pogrom
edged slightly into his rounded shoulders
It's 2011—
my running shoes
pour me across mountains and malls
glide me on the laminate synagogue floor
far far from hunger
my shoulders will not surrender
my hand extends in dance
to play

to toss off the sheitl of my great grandmother
to click "delete" on a few more minor notes
and then to carry my fiddle to the roof   ❧

Ardith Johnson

Beside the Highway

He called her "Honey," as if distracted
    by more important things
    like chopping weeds
    beside the highway.

She cooked, crocheted, grew children
    as if these mattered
    and began to sip
    a little more each day.

In time the warmth of wine
    froze all good hopes;
    dreams drowned
    in thirsty search.

And unseen weeds depleted
    hungry lives untended
    while highway's tidy path
    bypassed these stumbling travelers.   ❧

KATHAMANN

Beyond A Reasonable Doubt

Sappho's freckles deterred attitudes of sophistication. Chasing sheep in
Scotland is cosmic proof of unadulterated entrapment. Trained Amish
trap frogs in water reserves. *Amarita muscaris* mushrooms arouse
hormones from the far side. Erupting from the corner, a möbius
strip transfers into a solid hole. Archery prompts knee deep hope.

Cannons splat popcorn on the outskirts of the city. Toothpicks try
to emulate clothespins. The flight of a soul mate begrudged. A sieve
removes debris from wonder. Changing sides in the middle of a game
is bitter cold. A clean bathtub is as friendly as an aftertaste on the
tongue. A buffalo in the rain is sleek and chocolate. A sparkling back
becomes a rubbing limb.

Labrador Islands are full of sticky wood. The best excuse to see
is to imagine. Gleeful listening in a childlike emptiness. Behind
elation thanksgiving is extracted. Close to a shelter of connumbras.
Unlocking kinks in a system of spoiled people. Touching and chatting
everywhere is shifting the earth. An errant cripple full of saved past
participles.

You are a bundle of energy, always on the go.
Don't forget to do good deeds as you accumulate wealth.
A pleasant surprise is in store for you tonight.
Big things coming in future. Only matter of time.
Success is rarely created unless you're having fun at it.
Even the smallest candle burns brighter in the dark.
A man cannot be comfortable without his own approval.

A thrown stick landed in the sagging Spam. Round bruises enthralled in the defense of talk. An awesome candle spits out. The vacuum cleaner finally swallowed the cat. Wisdom in ditches disturbs private measure.

Misguided treats face the music between booze. Super pins bulging in miserable biscuits. Circles of evil in every croak of powder. A whiff of the status quo is like a superfluous gale on the plains. Scented oaks grow in Norwegian rows. The status of antlers on a Scottish wall. Laying down heavy in the dark. A backward vision where everything dissolves into flame. A guard on fire. Mix the food chain and the road.

My menopausal spread survives on Necco Wafers. Peering eyes through the crack where all are blessed in dreams of imagination and creativity. ๑

ZACHARY KLUCKMAN

Scrapbook for the Lonely

Start your canvas on photograph.
A black and white slide
of sea cliffs and birds on thin
electrical lines. One pair of shoes,
size six with the laces untied.

A sleeping woman with her hair
spilling loose across a table
where the wine bottle is corked
and the crackers, next to the cheese
are bundled in fancy tin.

Glue one cookie to the image
for texture. Excuse the dimensions,
raise a toast to her gloriously
red lips. Kiss her with a battery.
Cell phone, ion or lithium,
fully charged. Roll one ace bandage
around the canvas.
Her ankles will hurt from all the dancing.
Music moves her lips,

you can see it in that smile.
Embed one vinyl record
in the side of the frame
as if trying to jam a CD in
between the lovers whose kiss

stains the corner, below the Ford
Model T, the old man chewing
a licorice twist.

Time your walk to the saxophone
player, circumnavigate the whole,
canvas and frame, searching
for a moment out of place.   ❧

SARI KROSINSKY

Odysseus' abandoned crewman discusses Cyclops etiquette

after the Aeneid 3:758-952

Pour me some more o' that fine slop
you call wine, and I'll tell you a tale
to make you thank the gods
your worst trouble's a wooden horse.

Do you have any idea what it's like to spend
your days waiting to find out if you're
what's for dinner? Of course you don't.
Your captain knows when to run.

Stupid Odysseus couldn't even tie a knot.
Fell off the sheep near half a mile short
of the beach. Odysseus sailed off
heckling Polyphemus—once he got
a good league between 'em.

Bet he'll tell dear Penelope
how damn clever he was. Flesh-breath
hasn't been invited to any Cyclops parties
since he told 'em "no man" poked his eye out.
But Odysseus named himself true,
not clever. My captain is no

man. Sure, he can drag his soldiers

from safe harbor for a wild Cyclops chase,
but the way I see it, a captain leaving his men
behind is like a soldier dumping his shield.

I'll tell you what'd be clever—
not hoisting your sails
every time you hear there's a man-eating
Cyclops across the strait.

This draft's for Poseidon, strong drink
for a strong wave. I'll make a pact
with you, old man. Whoever finds
Odysseus first gets dibs
on sending him home to the fishes.   &

WAYNE LEE

Carrizozo Waitress

The waitress apologizes, says she's too young
to serve us beer, too uncoordinated to carry
two plates at a time so she can't serve us
all at once, doesn't smile because she wears braces.

This is Tammy's first time in the dining room.
Normally she cooks, washes dishes,
carries out the trash. She's been too busy
to clean the restrooms. She apologizes for that,

and for the Mexican Combo, which she thinks
is overdone. She wouldn't have cooked it so much,
she tells us as she refills our water glasses—
over the floor because she's afraid she'll spill
on the table. Because she's so uncoordinated.

By the time we decline the coconut layer cake
and choice of homemade pie, Tammy has told us
all about her miniature Schnauzer named Fuzzy,
the quarter horse she had to put down last year,
and her boyfriend Ryan who dumped her.
Because of the braces. She smiles anyway.   ✍

MARIETTA LEIS

Blue

spare paintings
sensuousness and formal order
nonobjective, reductive

mirroring, translucent

intense blueness, saturation
vast, unfathomable
hydration
quiet, pure, infinite, placid

whisper

lush lapping edges
ooze, melt
edginess
slices

pulsating

impacted edges
more beyond—continuum

oil paint—many layers, skins
nuances
descending deeply into the soul,
the core

peaceful, serene
repose
empty space—possibilities

stillness

e.e., Emerson
Cage

the fluid nature of our lives
inhaling, exhaling
between musical notes
pausing

now   ❧

CAROL LEWIS

Walking to Work

I pause on a foot-bridge of Japanese cedar
the click-clack of my footsteps silenced, a
river winds under the arch, green and
brimming, slim shadows probe a
current that braids and unravels—
In the blue morning, a kingfisher
bristles his ruff of water pearls
quivers on a willow's tip and dives—

I'm lying—the bridge is a flat,
concrete and asphalt job,
arterial traffic rumbles across—
No kingfishers, no willows; a raven
rummages in the eucalyptus searching
for birds' eggs, sparrows
fluff feathers in dust pools—

Ballona creek is a trickle in a
concrete trough, thin sheen of reflections
urging styrofoam, foil, algae, detritus
downstream—

A triad of ducks scoots under
the bridge, making the most of
a two-inch depth—   ❧

Maria Leyba

Collecting Names

Since she was ten
she's collected discarded
names flung out of school
windows by schoolteachers
believing Barrio children
needed white names
to make it in
America.

She's still pulling her
little red wagon filled
with beautiful Spanish
names up / down 4th Street,
Barelas / all over *Burque*
parading her precious cargo.

She wouldn't whisper
her name or let teachers
give her a new starched
one plucked off some
white clothesline
just unfurled her caged
tongue boiling with <u>anger</u>
screaming out her *nombre*
in her Mother Tongue
her *GRITOS* exploding
throughout the
Rio Grande Valley.

Those discarded names
got under her skin
wore her nerves down
still she needed them
for survival plucked
them off the ground
rolled them in her mouth
chewed / tasted them
played with incredible
sounds each one made
she was in love couldn't
live without her magical
names now alive in her.

The silver language
the pulse of her world
where her heart beats
with drums of ancient ones
where memories of
her *querencia* were
born.

If you listen carefully
the wind carries her
GRITOS of her
 collection of names
Ursula, Candelaria, Luciana,
Romola, Teodora, Maria Luisa,
Hilario, Anastacio, Pedro,
Ramon, Celestino, Domingo. ❧

GINA MARSELLE

hand-me-down

i stand quiet in line
my hands folded in prayer
holding a hand-me-down red glass rosary.
i'm waiting for communion.
i haven't been to confession or mass for months,
i came today because my soul is heavy.
inside St. Jude the air is dank,
smells from the flicker of cheap candles burning.
i feel unbalanced, easily distracted.
last night i hungered to wrap my nakedness
inside your skin for warmth,
but instead i folded into the arms
of a man i do not love.   ❧

MIRANDA MARSELLE

Night Sky

Night rests on the sky
hidden, dreaming happily
waiting to be seen. ❧

MARY MCGINNIS

Black Wind

Blame it on
Larry Goodell who revealed how
All his thoughts are going. When he's not
Concentrating, his mind becomes a tall and empty room for a
Kangaroo. And now, Lorca's coming, approaching me
With a smoldering cigar.
I just stand there with my basket of
Nothing. He's looking for a man in a
Dark suit to plan an assignation. With knitted
Black brows he stares into a
Lush corner but doesn't see
Anybody. I
Cry silently, Federico, a
Kangaroo stole my words.
Where will I go without words?
In a moment he will put out his cigar and nod,
Nod unsmiling in my
Direction, and neither of us will speak to each other again.   ✺

DON MCIVER

The Awning

A being capable of anything:
long drives without bathroom breaks,
driving around me on the basketball court,
asking for the Phillips head, flathead, crescent wrench, socket set
as I stumbled through the basic fixes,
unable to summon the patience
to read directions, pay attention,
to think before I acted.

Now, in a year when I actually worked on my car and made it better
     not worse,
to think that I would be the missing variable
in the equation of his retirement awning.
The obligatory grunt of muscle
as we lifted the beams.
I was the one who climbed up on the ladder,
who held the heavy, yet not unbearable weight above my head
and lifted up and over and down the post,
the crossbeam resting on both sides in position for the washer, bolt,
     washer, nut.
I was the able body, the patient mind, the driving force.

In the afternoon, I knew he was tired,
wanted to call it quits and disappear into a cold shower,
the leaning rock of recliner,
but I insisted.
Let's get as much done today as possible.

He plugged away, though watched me work more often than in the
    early morning hours.
And we did as much as we could with the materials at hand.
In a small town, 60 miles from the next bigger town,
we were stuck.
This suited him fine,
and I looked at the mass of wood, crossbeams, canopy pieces, bolts,
    hoists, nails,
and knew that I was strong.

I was the body that my brain could still abuse.
And my father, once capable of anything, was old.   🙤

MERIMÉE MOFFITT

Nativity

at birth she said "not mine"
you've brought a wrong child
dark eyes, black hair, red skin
changeling foreign but I see
Chief Joseph in every Rorschach
hand-stitching more comfortable
than French seams on Mama's Singer
I beaded moccasins sewed skins
rolled my own, brooms not vacuums
belly laughs not this dull captivity
I can't live in a city much more—but what
upgrade can I muster—the hard life?
that pioneer stuff?
no plan short of medicare likely
x-rays show it's getting late
one heart, one soul, one body
box of ashes
I carry my anger
heavy still as cannon balls
don't mess with me, just don't   ॐ

SAMUEL MOORMAN

Geography for Dummies

Pressed against a deli window
in old Oakland a world map shows
a German cockroach mashed in Siberia
at a blue bend of Lower Tunguska River—
where brown bug juice flows
east to the Yenisey before it empties
into Eniseisk Gulf and freezes
in the Arctic ice of Kara Sea

I'm chilling in drizzle on Grand Ave
tonight feeling old
and small watching giant peninsulas
bulge from this plate glass window—
Tamyr! Kanin! Yamal! Gidanski!
over little signs reading EGGS, MILK   ๖

YASMEEN NAJMI

Gulf Ghazal

On dry stripes between the feral bayous and rivers, they came to build, grow in thin places*. Life delivered in ritual tides, geologic gifts that oozed between plank floor toes, thin places.

The ashy, skirted frames of bald cypress and tupelo gum slumped like old women, dripped in antebellum lace of moss that filled dikes of sunlight, closed the thin places.

A fiery sun thundered to sky, eclipsed dark, earth's blood crept to shore staining, straining shells, wings, the sickled marsh grass - settled in all those thin places.

Thinking it was night again, eels left their watery nests among the breathing roots that held the world together, darting, twisting in the flow through thin places.

Fishermen, the anointed soldiers of Goddess Yemanja, pried the paralyzed from gluey graves, wound new levees like chastity belts around shores, dark clouds and truth spun below thin places.

Old Joe at Boutte's Bayou smiled, "Sorry, all I can fix you now is a beef poorboy sandwich. Cleanin' the oil is like gettin' gum off yo shoe," he cackled, missing teeth showed roux thin places.

His mouth slowly waned, Yasmeen, eyes fixed in a distant, smoky glaze, he said "The people in Lafitte or Theriot or anywhere round here, in these prowling bayous we know our thin places." ✒

* On public radio, a Louisiana native and naturalist mentioned the concept of a "thin place," a physical place on the landscape where the veil between this world and next is thin - a place you understand intuitively.

CAROL MOSCRIP

Shadows

It must have been
an anonymous tip
in a dream
that woke me

A whisper of light
drew me down the broad
generous staircase of that big Victorian house
where we lived in San Francisco during the war
– blackouts baffled me at the age of four
with the sudden flashes of star! star! star!
in the utter night as though pitched
into the sky by my fear of dark
and as we sat on my bed and listened for
the roaring sickening cosmic whistles of bombs,
Mother reminded me
that Father could see the same stars, too,
wherever he might be—

Late that night despite the dark
I tiptoed past Mother's pale floral
chair and Father's overstuffed one—
which meant his presence
and his absence through those years—
to peer from the shadows into a single shaft
of light casting its spot onto
the round mahogany table below

where Mother sat bolt upright
with an electrified stare
while Father held his head and wept,
just come home from war to find
the savings all spent

Scurrying in panic back upstairs,
I'd ducked under my blanket
lest he know I saw his tears –
then across my opening bedroom door,
the huge shadow of his anguish
stood there for a moment looking in
as I, curled up in my bed
like a shrimp on a platter,
pretended to be asleep
but peeking through my lashes,
bit down hard on my fear
of this big person in my house
crying like a child,
where would he sleep,
not here in my too small bed,
but after a silent moment he moved on,
and like any other child
distraught at night
he took refuge in my mother's room
where she would know how
to quiet his sobs, I knew
that I could not comfort him—
my first memory of him ever

The light of day did come
but could not bleach out that shadow

of the night before,
now permanent at my bedroom door
this solitude he brought home from war

That afternoon it was beer and cards
with the neighbors and he talked about
a swing set and a dog perhaps
for the backyard

I stood transfixed as if posed
for a photo, anxiously curious,
as I peered into the sunlit room
his shadow seated at the same place
now small upon the wall　　๑

BILL NEVINS

Bad News, a Waltz

Like speaking words of love to a bad drunk,
Batting a bear with a black-
iron fry pan
is decidedly
counter productive
it makes no dent
Or as the grizzly told Tim Treadwell
I ain't no metaphor man
were he simple vermin, beyond human pale
wolverine
or some snake tailed slithering giant New Guinea rat
and were you not already dead, Tim
even you
might set a sharp trap
snap his scrawny back
like UB40 ska-jive—
stag o lee neck snap—
simple as that
But he's
Grizz, man,
long gone gray
grumpy in moods
brave enough in his day
rears up on hind legs
still
now and then
plays deadly chess with Tony Hopkins

if you credit movie hype
bearded, big-shouldered, brawny, hirsute
and oh so tragically stupidly
male—
what that cool Kraut cinemage
saw safe behind time and a long lens
cold-eyed Grizzer red in tooth and claw,
Pilgrim,
basso profundo rumbling
snuffling
growling, piss drunk
shambles
through
our kitchen at night
lonely enough to gobble a man
whole
cough, curse, crash into her table
the kid's high chair
howl out my name, your name, his wife's name, mine,
cracking her new glass coffee pot.
Of course he never meant--
how could a bear mean?—
any of it
at all at all
in morning light
just trying to get sober
enough
shuffles big feet
slurps black java
scalding
so cuddly when he's sweet
big dark bear

his ragged yellow hooked paw
groping for chips,
cold pizza
hand rolled tortillas
all that rich hot food she'd put
away in the fridge hours back
when he didn't come home
all garbage to him now
well fit for him to eat
snuffling through it all
while she pulled a stoic blanket over ears
not to hear
that damned bear
in her pantry
once again

How to mend the damage done?
Buy her a steel Mr. Coffee carafe
dog house roses
join AA, find God
get a job
take her out for truffle fries and fine white wine?

Yet how to get that bear out of her kitchen?
Ever?
He ain't no Teddy. No Papa.
He ain't no Pooh.
He ain't one bit funny
and he damned well can't be YOU!

How to forget terror?
How do you get bear outta kitchen?

Don't shoot the poor damn bear.
Just never let the bastard back in. ❧

BRUCE NOLL

In Place

And the great horned owl
calls in the hollow

from the window awakened
I can see the moon on

its westward decline behind
the winter skeleton of the

hackberry   all is still
across the meadow of snow

the ears of the cottontail
in the cattail thicket

are still as ice   still as
the field mouse burrowed

in its tunnels of grass
beneath the drifts   still

as my wide wonder for
this silent gift of crystalline   ❧

MARY OERTEL-KIRSCHNER

Rue Jacob

It's been slipping into my mind again—
an ordinary time, at the time.
Now it pops back at odd moments,
still bringing inordinate stings of pleasure.

I was twenty-six and had come up from the south by train,
a chunk of Camembert ripening in my pack, oozing and pungent.
I found the hotel on Rue Jacob, a room on the second floor,
spacious and spare,
overlooking the street
where the sounds from a lively market rose up
and awakened me early.

I went down for crusty bread and fresh crunchy peppers,
took them back to my perfect room. It was
everything I needed.

Forty years later I walked the length of Rue Jacob
but found no trace, no market, no old hotel.

I have it only in my mind,
big bed in the corner,
warm shouts from the vegetable stalls,
me, secure and free,
everything I wanted.   ֍

JILL A. OGLESBY

Geimhreadh*

Here is the gray shield of sky.
Here are the fields, yellow and plowed
in thick clod rows, waiting for spring,
like the raked yellow carpet in rooms I've left,
where I've removed furniture, the walls
gray-spackled, empty.

I could be standing in the window
of one of them now, sunlight diffuse
through curtains sheer as clouds,
wearing a green apron over a blue summer dress.
Twenty seven, water boiling on the stove for pink shrimp
I'll cook with yellow corn and red cayenne

as my neighbor instructed, under the magnolias
when I drove her to the welfare office.
She told me a cat could steal the breath of a baby.
Her children played in my rented front yard.
We compared our skins, theirs
earth rich and chocolate, mine leche con leche,
strange, other. Shocking, a little disgusting—
you could see the green veins through it.

Her children have grown and gone.
I've grown and gone back home.
This valley is the palm of a hand that holds me;
the Rio Grande passing through it

is a green vein passing through my wrist.
Out the car windows, the county huddles in winter cold.
Here, where the evil eye might still harm a child.

Driving through the Pueblo, past the casino—
a piggy bank on the hill, full of silver change—
Time is breath fog in the air.
Time is nests made visible in bare winter trees.
Light of the short winter day shifts through the glass.
Gravity pulls the car inward, a tether.
Winter is beyond regrets, beyond memories.　　☙

* "Geimhreadh" means "Winter" in Irish.

Marilyn O'Leary

Drought

The less water, the more tears
until there can be no more tears,
only dust.
The helplessness of drought—
furrowed rows, expectant
blown to flatness.

Sand scratches on the tin roof
pits the window pane—
spider webs appear, but no
drops of dew hover on the filaments.

Dry lightning ignites flames.
Where is the water to quench this fire?
The river is dry.
We have built our homes on sand.   ❧

KATE PADILLA

New Mexico Heirloom

It was decades past
a crisp September
father buys green chiles
in a gunny sack
from the *chilero*
at the Wyoming Texaco

In our backyard
he shouts "sonie-bitchie"
at vanishing grill coals
he pours more lighter fluid
flames roar   then die

Mother moans
fate slams against her will
she'll roast chiles
in her always spotless oven

Shawled shoulders round
her exiled hands peel chiles
blackened skins resist
just bits and pieces
a taste of home.   ❧

Scott Palmer

Bukowski Suicide

Charles on twitter, strong
a striped dragon in flames

He is in Slow burn down
mode, always deconstructing
The old patriarch drunk lord foul,

I hear the cell phone bastard
----disconnect-----

Ten hours later, Michael Thomas
coffee fresh in my veins, cell vibrates

Close to my ruin of thighs,
Bru again; on the record

feverish about neighborhood
Girls body and breasts budding;

Rain Gods come to LA
purify Bukowski in acid rain

he walks on the beach
a bearded poet & prophet

As I record him digital with
My new one shot camera

to record him for posterity
I avoid the sandy potholes,

between him and the
legal ocean spray.

Get his every thought on video,
writing poems on the DVD case.

a book of my Bru poems,
Charles walking on water

Hours later after the beach
I high on a caramel frappe,

I am abuzz, the cell phone rings
Outside raindrops pelt hard ground

The drops are like computer keys
spelling out a new sky saga

rip gnash holes in the spring garden,
Charles voice throbs with lust again

He talks about a twenty year old Virginia,
An aspiring starlet face as lovely as day,

With a body as hard as night
He loves her, God! Not Again

He whines whimpers, needs my help
To be the honey to attract the worker bee

Another unstoppable mudslide.
Her hands are so delicate,

the better to trap you with Charles
in addictions in Los Angeles, today, anyway,

He has new poems about her, to share
A sigh in the other room.

He is convinced she is unhappy.
He must elate her with greenbacks,

Never enough---
She comes back for more.

She wants hundreds, not just ones.
He says yes.

a week later, I have not heard from him.
There are news reports everywhere.

Bukowski found in the nude.
A Beam bottle in his dead hands.

She calls me.
I am sick in the can.

I listen through the shower.
She is in the water ... wants hush money.

I tell her to look in the pockets
in her faded blue jeans   ✇

ANNMARIE H. PEARSON

Sister Josephine

The woman stood tall against the wee-small
children of parochial school.
A nun by trade, she ruled by fear
and the pointed blade.
Innocent youth shook with fright
when her steps stopped by their desk,
there they froze statuesque.

Sister Josephine, why were you so mean?

She wore a long black robe with a tall white habit,
a witch she could be, for bewitched she was to me.
Anger protruded from her lips,
her fists, and her swatting hands.
No one escaped her bitter cruel plight.
A canonized saint she would never be.
However, she always prayed for the sinner in me.

Sister Josephine, why were you so mean?

Our prayers were never heard,
as we feared her every word.
Each day she strolled through the aisles
carrying her necromancer's wand;
ready to strike if you did not respond.
Alert we all were with intent and mindful of her lessons.
Her class was always first, she never settled for second.

Her students could withstand,
for she believed they were from the Promised Land.

Sister Josephine, why were you so mean?

The year was finally over
and cheers were harkened with delight.
We all passed fourth grade and freedom was in sight.
But to our chagrin, we did not win.
We all heard Sister Josephine had advanced a level.
Mother Superior gathered us around,
"My darling little angels, Sister Josephine
is fifth grade bound."
We all stood dumbfound,
not another year with Sister Josephine.

We all rebelled even with the dread of hell,
but we knew we were stuck
as fifth grade went amuck.   ❧

CHARLES POWELL

Begging Eyes

Men, women, boys, girls
They struggle hard
Desperate to sell things
From large live snails
To boiled chicken eggs
And salty fish jerky
From cotton socks
To assorted T-shirts
And colorful dresses
And from towels
To coveted flashlights
And precious toilet paper

They try so very hard
Hawking their goods
Seeking to persuade
They attempt reasoning
Charming, shaming
Anything for a sale
They don't take no for an answer
They test different styles and words
Different facial expressions
They repeat themselves
Follow tourists
Even take hold of a sleeve or hand

There are others wanting charity
The elderly, the infirm
The down and out
In wheel chairs, on crutches
Blind or extremities deformed or missing
Hobbling after visitors
Hands open and extended
Requesting a little something to help
—Something—anything!
And then there're those eyes
Those sad eyes
Pleading eyes

At the markets, at the tourist attractions
Almost everywhere you go
The hawkers are there
Vending their wares--
Artwork, jewelry, maps
Even little plastic bags of water
If traffic slows or stops
They're there to wash windshields
Plead for handouts or peddle things
And then there're those eyes
There're always those eyes
Asking eyes, accusing eyes

Accusing me of having so much
Accusing me of having an easy life
Of having clothing I don't wear
More food and apartment space than I need
Of having a computer, a mini-van, and three TVs

Accusing me of polluting and poisoning
Taking more than I require
Using more than my share
And those eyes, always those eyes
Crying eyes without tears
Questioning eyes, imploring eyes
Forever those eyes   ଈ

Robert Reeves

Here Be Dragons

Boylady Ladyboy,
I think you shot testosterone for those couple months
not just to sup the best of both worlds
but land on a wild shore that would be you,
your own. You hung back
from the cliff of Man,
that drop off the flat earth into the white shriek
peopled with fixed star and God.
You put the ampule away.
It still sweats a tinkle at the bottom.

You engineered a photo of yourself
as both sexes (was the concept.
Not a success)—in the right panel
you came out a surly dyke, in the left
this frivolous creature nowhere known on earth.
If those are the options,
I get your lust for difference.

The doctors are taking me
to that mariner's region between the genders,
the hideous gap on the chart.
No hope, given the iron smile of science,
that we can meet there,
hail and pass in the faery mists ...
but last night in our mingle and our loss
I glimpsed the coast of a New World
replete with unimagined gold. ✎

ELIZABETH ROLL

The Quarter

leaving Antoine's
onto Rue Saint Louis
Oysters Rockefeller
rumbles in my belly
the residue of Peach Melba
lingers on my tongue

strolling down Rue Bourbon
black satin tight swish sultry
strutting past
Creoles' Cajun kitchen
strip joints   hustlers
the aroma of gardenias
mingle with twangs
of praline hawkers

heat of the city
pouring into out of my pores
hot   honey   rum   running
through whispering veins
a dreamwalk through the Quarter
abuzz with sizzling jazz

black musicians jive
blusterous trios
trumpet trombone sax
blare   wail   growl

as the sleek singular clarinet
emerges out of smoky mist
with a clear savory tune

the bassist slams
picks his taut wiry strings
the piano player
levitates in jubilation

chocolate fingers
ride up and down ivory
black shiny skin
pock puddled in sweat
a wide white flaring grin
laced in Voodoo and Saints

the swell of the crescent river
drives me down Rue Ann
to Jackson Square
at the Cathedral
I cross myself

a quarter or two
to the last slapping boys
beating out rhythm
on skinny legs
shuffling zippy feet

4 a.m. Café Du Monde
slip off shoes
stretch toes on cement

watch day laborers
join denizens of the night

jazz players   pimps
hookers   bartenders
busboys   cooks
farmers bringing produce
to the market
fishermen bringing in
the catch from Belle Rose
nuns picking up provisions
for orphanages   schools
restaurateurs purchasing
food for the budding day

joined together
with fingers white
from powdered beignets
dipped in black-chicory coffee
blended with steamy milk

one rhapsody ends
a new opus begins
in the French Quarter   ✼

BONNIE RUCOBO

My Mother's Brother

He prayed at the synagogue
Every morning, dovening in his white
Yarmulke and talis.
He and I performed the unveiling service
At my father's grave site,
Reading the prayers in Hebrew and English.
I took the part of the rabbi, he the cantor.
I took care not to plant
My feet directly on the frozen grave;
He stood on the grave site without hesitation.
At the close of the service a monument in granite
Was unsheathed.

It was not his work that made him smile
But the pirouettes he played on the clarinet
That he meticulously cleaned and shined.
He produced a sound molasses-thick
As he blew on the horn that reverberated
Through his small house.
He marched in the Redskins Band,
And was a regular with a local
Dixieland combo.

He was buried at the beginning
Of the blizzard of the century,
The rabbi chanting the "El Maleh Rachamim,"
The prayer for the departed

Who are holy and pure of heart.
The snow spilled down,
Blanketing the grave site and
The family praying in chairs under a white tent
Soon camouflaged in the whirling snow.   ✎

GEORGIA SANTA MARIA

Ojito Arroyo (for Mary)

Ojito arroyo sparkles at eleven, like the Taj Mahal
White, like gypsum. White, like bone.
A studded trail up Truchas Mountain
To the top's white snows.

There, along the bank, ghosts live, and I remember
Moonlight on the cobwebs, silver spider knows,
And keeps her secrets. There's a whisper
Amongst the cottonwood castanets
Gold autumnal dancing, a gust of wind, perhaps,
Caressing stones.

Here we danced too, bare feet along the ditch bank.
Celebrated corn, as cruel cedars watched, silent
They bide their time. They know
That only they will last, forever. Yet, still,
There is a memory of songs, a memory of living
All the daily stuff of boredom going sour. Sex
And the humming of insects, barely audible
And unbearably oppressive.

Trying to crack the fruit jar for its honey,
Crawling round the lip, an echoing drone
Of buzzing, buzzing. And, finally, then
A sweeter meat. It's owner lying in her own
Jellied fluids, become an artifact.
A relic of her time.

History repeats its horror
In the memory of the peach tree.
As they looked on, the pinon said
"I told you so." Then, harrumphed and shrugged.
The canyon can't forget, and neither can the wind,
Bound to babble up and down, Up and down.
The corn grows tired and withers, brown.
In rustling rasping argument, she
Scrapes the ground in grief, the only mourner.
Though, memory's promise
Will repeat the scene.

Ojito Arroyo sparkles at eleven
Like the Taj Mahal.
White like gypsum
White like bone. ☙

Daniel Schwartz

Necropolis

Think like a mountain
Be a forest
Feel the ocean
See everything
Want nothing
Find peace with nature
Deep within the heart
The peace of the cemetery
Is no peace at all
The love of death
Is no great love
The celebration of life
Is not the way of the bomb
And how some love bombs
Enough is never enough

Rain light shadow wind
Bless me save me
From Los Alamos
War planes
War ships
War toys
The crime of war
Militarism
The self righteous
Full of hubris
Nature will always have the final word

Tell the truth
Make miracles happen
Create beauty
Love everything that is innocent
The force of life is vast and strong
See it feel it breathe it in
Hold your breath   ❧

ELAINE SCHWARTZ

Paseo en El Paso, 1945

Pushing the dark blue baby carriage
Miriam strolls through the *Plaza Central.*

Olive toned hands firmly grasp
the warm metal handle.
Black hair gently caresses the red peonies
embroidered upon the collar
of her beige linen suit.
Engorged breasts strain the buttons
of the jacket.

The hot Texas spring
challenges this midwestern bride.
Her feet, in fashionable pre-war pumps,
begin to swell. She finds relief
on the Spanish tile bench
encircling the alligator pool.

Miriam adjusts the baby's lace bonnet.
Brown eyes focused on her daughter's blue ones,
she doesn't notice the approach of the woman.

What a happy baby! So clean and fresh!
You take her for a stroll every afternoon?
You are a fine nanny.
I have two little ones at home.

I could use your services.
I'll pay you well.

Miriam smiles,
raises her head, momentarily
shifts her gaze to the woman.
Thank you.
I'm happy with my current employer.   ❧

Lauren Schwartz

Acropolis

Walking
      uphill, upwind
we swallow the dust that rises from the ruins.

We walk
      Pam, Michal, and I
with the intricacy of our own steps,
like small children, cautiously crossing the room
from mother to father for the first time.

We walk
      uphill in order to stand on top
of this very old, very dusty city that smells
like fading yellow paper. The type my grandfather
wrote poems on as a young Marine—the ones I keep in a box.

The day appears to have no sky—
      up here thin air fills our lungs
and yet our lungs are heavy with this thin air.

(The thickness of breathing—the difficulty
of reading old poems on brittle paper.)

I consider the heat of the sun—
I imagine it is the flare of Achilles' shield
bearing down, giving birth to
flowers and shadows and nations.

I breathe the dust
of bone and blood and flowers.
Pam, Michal and I reach the top.

Looking downhill
        I see shadows of war,
armor and horses of men, but no men.
The vision of riderless horses,
scattered bones of men and rams and ewes,
small bits of dried flowers, broken shadows,
and something like hope, mingle low to the ground.
The vision is uplifted as dust in a breeze
veiled in the white glint of Achilles' shield.
The vision like a childhood past, or the memory
of our first steps is obscured by the dust.

Looking downhill
I imagine warriors and feasts
and fields of flowers, the smell of fresh blood;
but the day is white and the shield, engraved
with stories of the world protects me
from the taste of fresh spilled blood. It is
imagination drifting with the dust
                        Uphill
                                upwind.

And with each dry white swallow of breath,
the ancient columns splinter like bones—I smell no blood
I smell only my grandfather's poems.
All I can know is the taste of dust
of bones and flowers.   ✜

BEATLICK JOE SPEER

Glad to Be

Jody and Doris went for a stroll
she turned incandescent
at the sight of a Thrift Store sign.
While she rummaged bargain bins
Jody considered his fate,
he had been diagnosed
with pancreatic cancer
and informed by an
oncologist that his
lifeline would soon unravel.
He saw a woman in a wheelchair
with banners and balloons
floating behind her
she seemed happy and resolute.
He fantasized changing bodies with her,
he could no longer hike
the mountain trails
but maybe it would add
a few bonus hours
to his time sheet.
He saw a blind man
plodding along with a probing pole,
if they could swap places
he would have to cancel
his Netflix account
but it might extend his days.
He saw a healthy young man

strutting along in a marine uniform
supremely capable of climbing
Mount Shasta with
a hundred-pound rucksack.
Jody viewed the American military
as a self-justified terrorist group
but if he could tote a gun
he might live long enough
to retire with benefits.
Doris appeared with her sack
which included a lotion to keep
her face wrinkle free
and youngishly smooth.
"Let's walk for a spell," she suggested
"and we'll return to our
cozy nook and a bowl
of chowder and barley."
Jody held her hand
and considered how lucky
he was to have a loving caregiver.
He remembered an uncle
who had a brain tumor
and the family finagled
to find him a place to die.
Doris cooked for Jody
helped him bathe
and catered to his every whim.
Jody decided not to be
a woman in a motorized chair
her accelerator might stick
and she'd be crushed
in traffic.

The blind man might
fall down a staircase
and break his spine.
The soldier will probably
return for another tour
of duty in Afghanistan
and get blasted by a
roadside bomb and die
while deluding himself
he was fighting for freedom.
Jody realized he was glad
to be himself and to have
time to prepare for the
next major life transition.   ❧

Marilyn Stablein

Curing the Bones

In Tivoli near the Hudson
I picked from the mud
three dozen winged locust shells
left behind when spineless grubs
dug down for their seventeen year sleep.

Those carapace shells, dried seed
pods, and red earth fill glass jars
in my studio. Assemblages house
aged bones, skulls, bugs, dismembered
doll's limbs. River rocks, wild herbs,
line the window sills.

Musical bones: Tibetan monks
blew trumpets made from thigh bones;
carved human skulls into ritual
offering bowls. Paper and sugar
skulls adorn Day of the Dead shrines
in Juarez and Corrales.

When an artist friend, Gail, moved
from her Catskill studio she gave
me a wasp's nest, sea shells, dried
insects resting on cotton beds and a large
hog's skull she boiled for days
until the meat fell off the bone.

I set the glossy skull to cure
in a humid New York summer.
After a month black fungus settled
over the bone like monsoon mold
on shoe leather. On really hot humid
days grease, oil and sap of bone,
seeped out, stained the porch.

Three years passed; fangs fell out.
The skull still cures. In dreams I haunt
a high desert studio: hot dry winds,
relentless sun, every bone a brittle white.   ❧

K. K. (KITTY) TODOROVICH

At Auntie's Viewing

How we polished with vinegar and oil
to keep the cheap green off lamps
and the coffee table's tacked-on brass trim.
Now it rims your new box.

Rats scratched at the wall behind the bed
where I cried my first married night
in the black attic of my new husband's mother's.
During an Ossabaw storm, the house, propped up on bricks,
lifted its flimsy hide to show God
the dank slumping stacks of string-tied boxes
betraying an earlier bride.

The house originally was a barn
Like the one my father grew up in.
His barn, like a castle, stood dead center in the onion field.
Ten living kids, grandpa, grandma, Auntie with somebody else's kids
And in winter the dogs, the workhorse, mousers and milk cow.

Casket brass is real. Still, half of life
is darkness. A division
of the indivisible.

We learn by touch and tears
to exist within it and without it
learn with that part of ourselves

we call on instead of the money
that shines for so few.

It's how we recover faith. ❧

SAL TREPPIEDI

One Moment Past Midnight

I want to dance like tomorrow is an afterthought
Find joy in the hues of sunrise and sunset
I want to pick pennies off the ground and make wishes
fling them into the air and spread the luck
I want to stare at a digital clock
as it turns one moment past midnight
scream with unbridled moxie
run naked through the streets yelling
"HERE I AM"
until a caravan of sweet carnal knowledge cascades into utopia
I want to turn the page of the calendar
and know that there are thirty more opportunities to live life to the
fullest
and you, February, I'll stop time to get the most of two less days
I want to pick fruit with my teeth
I want to touch until we conjure metaphors and celebrate secrets
I want to make up the rules as we go along
break them because we can
dirty my hands molding them back together   ✎

Aaron Trumm

Walking Dead

I am walking dead today
mother of six three taken away

and though there are hours of burning sand
the cradle of civilization cannot warm my hands
they are cold from the touch of death
and long to cradle sons' foreheads
they are withered from three souls gone far from my body
they float
as if they loved still

and far from the sun and the sand and the sky
my sons lie on crumpled army cots
and wonder why the desert never lies

I am walking dead today
all my hands can do is pray

and sometimes I wonder if Allah will not listen to daughters

I am bathing in the darkness
the sky is stars and rain and everything in between
I am looking for my headstone
staying clean like stone and rain
I am cold mother shunning her daughters
I am starving
listening to Allah scream and boom and gleam

throwing things on Constantinople and Babylon

my hands are looking for something to touch
but they don't want daughters
they don't want fathers
they don't need a blanket or a pen or a phone
they need SONS
don't take my SONS
I am walking dead today
my sons are my SOUL

but Islam's sons are lined up like grains of sand
they blow away before the night comes
and crazy, desperate birds from the other side of hell
come steady now
every night
when I can't sleep anyway

they drop wind and word and nothing for nothing
and sons,
they send no word of aliveness or grief
they say no prayer to their mother
they send nothing home unless ashes
and letters with news
not of heroism, heat and death
only villains
and victims

they only send letters here, if your sons are dead

I am walking dead today
mother of six three taken away

I pray to the new morning dust and the sun
that I may never hear
that I may take my faith into the old side of the city
and rejoice at knowing nothing

I have bled six placentas into the Earth for you, Allah
I have borne your word and want

let me hear nothing,
if silence be the word of triumph

let me see no man again for all my days
as long as no corpse be given to me in the evening
fresh with the smell of blood and lead

I am walking dead today
no everything is NOT ok
I am like all mothers with bullets in their bellies
sons waiting in Allah's place
begging to be birthed
so they can walk this fair firm Earth in their skins
falling in their fathers' footsteps
deepened by the ages of want and sin so now they're foxholes
slobber
dripping
gushing
bleeding
everything naked
everything in the skin
standing in their dirty dripping holes
waiting for rain
why?

I am bloodier than the dust
walking dead brained in the wind
waiting for the dry-eyed sky to cry my sons to me
mother of six three taken away

it only rains here, when you're dead   ❧

Bob Warren

Sonny

In the very early days,
He'd been a contract writer.
And if he'd done what he was supposed
To do when he was supposed to do it,
Nobody ever would have heard of Marvin Gaye.
Instead he married another writer,
Had two kids, got divorced, and another job,
And sang with his sister Mary
Who played piano, and his brother Al
Who played bass, in the afternoons,
After work, in the front room
Of their Mother's three family flat,
With first floor French windows that opened
To a small porch and a ghetto yard filled
On warm summer afternoons and nights
All the way across the street, with people
Who came to hear, through those windows,
The best music they would hear in years
Or maybe ever.
          Late of an afternoon,
I was trying to get through the crowd,
Up the stairs, and a guy asked me
What the fuck I was doing,
And Sonny stuck his head
Out the window, and said,
"He lives here." From then on,
There were no problems,

And young Whitey X rolled on through
Like Moses at the Red Sea.

Now, forty-five years later,
Mary dead twenty-plus years
From cancer, and Al about to die,
Sonny and I talk on the phone
Every couple of months -
Two old men with the gimps
Old men have, with the distances
Of time and the heartbeats
Only survivors can claim.
He wakes, as I do, each morning,
With the thought, the hope,
That while this ain't heaven,
It sure as hell ain't hell.

And somehow, again,
If only in these memories,
Sister Mary's left foot is again shoeless,
And her bare heel is stomping the beat
On the wooden floor, hard and strong,
And powerful, and Brother Al
Is playing bass with his controlled
And contented four string mania,
And Sonny is singing from a heart so big
It makes grown men almost cry
At the beauty of it. And I am still
The watching ghetto white kid
Too crazy to mess with.
And a whole world, a whole world,
Is filled with joy, the joy,

The joy and the beauty of every single
Moment of that time.
And there ain't a god damned thing wrong
With a crazy old man
For the membrance of that memory. ✌

The Writing Class

Patty passed around copies of herself,
her handwritten assignments. I swear
I could see the pressure of her pencil
on the words "unfair" and "torture".

Her brothers drank and fought
at the kitchen table, shooting
at anything that moved; stopping only
to regroup for another verbal attack

on some Anglo *pendejo*,
the family always taking sides.
Patty lived in Spanish, labored in English
to find a voice strong enough

to put an end to it,
big enough to nurse them all.
I wanted to give her more words,
a machine gun with verbs,

windows, ventilation in her kitchen.
I wanted to dynamite that table,
burn it with description,
destroy it with alliteration,

but every week she brought us back
to that fist rattling the dishes.

Her pages, like the splattered wall
behind her stove, were decorated

with crucifixion and blame
where she pressed her ten-line poems
into *tortillas*, thin as torn flesh—
ladling up the meat of the matter. ✌

RICHARD WOLFSON

Broken Time

When every end is broken,
the mist of butterfly regret,
scarcity of decision, dependent on inherited hope.

The chill that materializes on half-eaten mountains,
fragile eternity, softness like soap sparrow,
the divisibility of art, placed upon the tomb.

When nectar is countenanced in triangulation,
clumps of mud, showered like patient monks,
the vector of invisibility in vacuous memory.

The past snorts in a frozen holler,
Darwin's spit enshrined in chocolate museum,
Guards flit like a doorway apprentice.

The clown of tolerance drowning in murky air,
shoulders drift in popsicle music
that claps ere the beginning be broken.   ❧

JASON YURCIC

Winter in the Desert

Sweet nectar drips
from peach pit sun
hanging over frozen vast land
No one dares the cold
Fingers pounding like glancing hammer blows
on flesh tip piano keys
have left them numb
They sound the out-of-tune alarm
"Get inside, you asshole. It's -12 degrees!"
But I love the pain
Spinning car tires
People without heat
A state of emergency has been declared
on this cold, cold day
Growing stalactites of nectar from eave of roof glisten as they reach
for the earth
Shoveling snow soft as powdered sugar
Fingers pounding
Peach pit nectar of sun
Frozen, frozen
But I can see tulip bulbs waiting in the shade
in the hard earth
-12 degrees
Wind is howling its coyote song of loneliness
while children sleep
unaware of another day off of school
But I am here reading windswept-snow-drift-braille

and trying to taste an early spring
In my mind
the flowers lay waiting
flowers within
Flowering within me on this cold day
is the gratitude I possess
for having survived my crazy life
with my soul intact
And only the red earth knows my pain
And the flowers
And the flowers
And the flowers ...   ✺

Contributors

Arun Ahuja,
MS in biomedical engineering, currently studies Tai Chi at UNM. He teaches qigong and is developing awareness movement exercises for diabetes. Arun's work appears in *Conceptions Southwest* (editor's pick, fiction), *Planet magazine* (online), *The Rag* and *Central Avenue*, plus a few letters in *Weekly Alibi* and *Daily Lobo*.

Timothy B. Anderson
is a writer/photographer. His writing has spanned many genres, including the forthcoming book, *Frame of Mind* (poetry) and *Poser: a sketchbook of ideas for artists and models*. He has photographed in many areas, specializing in fine-art nudes and portraiture. cygnetpress.com

Priscilla Baca y Candelaria
Farmer, painter, poeta, her bilingual poetry has appeared in many magazines, anthologies, chapbooks and cds. This retired teacher has taught poetry workshops, published many magazine articles and performed her poetry across the USA, in Mexico and in the films *Alamo Viejo* and *Committing Poetry in Times of War*.

Chandra Bales
is a developing writer, and has a passion for mathematics and language. A member of the Albuquerque Word Weavers and New Mexico State Poetry Society, she feels fortunate to be among such friendly and knowledgeable writers. Chandra lives with her husband in the East Mountains.

Hakim Bellamy
is a father, fighter for good causes, lover, honorable mention recipient of the Paul Bartlett Ré Peace Prize, student, journalist, fútbol addict, song-writer, fledgling actor, youth poetry groupie, and National Poetry Slam Champion who sometimes likes to get published and wishes he traveled more. www.hakimbe.com

Shirley Balance Blackwell
won the Amy Kitchener Foundation's 2010 New Mexico Senior Poet Laureate Award. She serves as chancellor of the NM State Poetry Society and recently rewrote its constitution. Poetry is her antidote to a (past) career of analytical writing and editing.

Sandi Blanton
is a sometimes poet, writer and painter and a full-time gardener and seeker of peace and quiet. She lives in Albuquerque, NM.

Joanne Bodin,
a retired Albuquerque teacher of gifted students, received her Ph. D. in Curriculum, Instruction and Multicultural Teacher Education. Her novel, *Walking Fish* (2011) has been nominated for literary awards. She is working on a book of poetry entitled: *Piggybacked and Other Poems*. Joanne plays jazz piano and paints water colors.
www.walkingfishnovel.com

Benjamin Bormann's
poetry concentrates on the role of Place in humanity's quest for understanding. As such, he draws attention to the connections between the land, the wildlife, the weather, and both the individual and social responsibilities of belonging that humans hold regarding all of these things.

Joe Bottone
Poetry came to me as a gift I took for granted, abused, abandoned
its longing for expression so I was cursed with its haunting. Several
years now, my vow fixed and holy, there is no other life for me; not just
poetry but poetry illumined, lustrous conscious of its mystic soul.
www.joebottonepoet.com

Rich Boucher
has published four chapbooks of poetry and, for seven years, hosted
a poetry slam in Newark, Delaware. A twisted heart and a homeless
mind. His poems have appeared in *Adobe Walls: An Anthology of New
Mexico Poetry*, *The Rag*, *Clutching at Straws*, *Shot Glass Journal*, and
Mutant Root.

Karin Bradberry,
Albuquerque poet, teacher and visual artist, enjoys creating "poetry
shrines," sculptures which embody her poems. She co-edits/publishes
the Rag. Karin has won numerous poetry prizes, has been published
in local and national magazines as well as several anthologies, and has
twice been Fixed and Free's featured poet.

Debbi Brody
is an avid attendee and leader of poetry workshops throughout the
Southwest. She has been published in numerous journals, magazines
and anthologies of note. She is currently working on her newest full
length poetry manuscript.

Gary L. Brower
has taught at various universities, published three books and a CD of
poetry, is editor of the *Malpais Review* and is a director of the Duende
Poetry Series of Placitas. Forthcoming are: *Leaving Cairo* (with photos
and CD) and a CD, *In Paradise We Will Become Music.*

Billy Brown
Following three decades loathing poetry, Billy began writing
poems for self-healing after his daughter Elizabeth was killed in a
one-car crash in 1996. The intimacy of sharing deep feelings grants
permission to others to share theirs. Billy organizes monthly poetry
readings, quarterly poetry Open Houses and reads poetry daily.

Lauren Camp
is the author of *This Business of Wisdom* (West End Press, 2010). She
is also an accomplished visual artist and radio host. Her poems have
appeared in *Leveler, dirtcakes, Hotel Amerika, New Verse News* and other
journals, and she has received honors from the Gaea Foundation and
Recursos. www.laurencamp.com

Gregory L. Candela
is a professor emeritus at UNM and has resided in New Mexico since
1972. He holds a doctorate in American literature from UNM and
taught creative writing there. Recent publications include poems in the
Harwood Anthology, Central Avenue, the Rag, Malpaís Review and *Adobe
Walls.*

Gary S. Chorre
is an Oscar Butler P.H.I.T. fitness enthusiast. He recently attended
a Haganah (Israeli Special Forces) self-defense conference in Las
Vegas, NV., from which he is finally recovering. He collects Civil War
memorabilia. The poetry scene was once a joy and performing still is
invigorating.

Dee Cohen
is a new resident of Albuquerque. Her poems have been published in
various journals on and off line. Her chap book *Lime Ave Evening* was
published by the Laguna Poets.

Carlos Contreras,
two-time national performance poetry champion, is lead facilitator
of the Voces Writing Institute, at the National Hispanic Culutural
Center, winner of the Bravos Excellence in Literary Arts Award. A
poet, educator, mentor, artist and human being, Carlos is author of *A
Man In Pieces: Poems for My Father* (2008).

Deborah Coy
has loved words since the first time she was read *Winnie The Pooh.*
They are her playthings, and sometimes they can be built into poetry.

Susy Crandall
Itchin' to write, to scrape the painfully unexpressed off internal organs
and lay it out in fresh air and sunshine to heal, where sharing fraction-
ates pain. Scrubbing out the last of my angst cabinets to fill with love
and light, to live, a worker among workers, a friend among friends.

Sylvia Ramos Cruz
is a physician and surgeon who lives in Albuquerque and loves words
for what they can do. Her goal is to use the fewest words possible to
recount a moment born in her own experience but able to embrace
anyone's life. She is not yet there.

Julie Dunleavy
is a poet living in Albuquerque, New Mexico. Her poetry is included
in *Quartet; Colors*, a chap book; and *Haunted*, a recently published book
with photographer, Richard Ruddy.

Bill Epler
My PhD is in mathematics, but poetry never fails to refresh and
balance my spirit. How else can we stay connected with the transcen-
dental whiffs that are never there when we look at them directly? I
also have two daughters who are poetry incarnate to me.

Mary Fogarty
lived in several countries as resident and exchange student. Exposure
to varied cultures inspired her as an activist, public speaker, teacher,
publisher, author, sculptress and painter. She has published six books
of poetry, short stories and essays, available on Amazon.com, and has
won both national and international contests.

Elizabeth Ann Galligan
finds inspiration in the beautiful diversity of people and landscapes of
the Southwest. Her poetry celebrates relationships and gives tribute
to entities greater than oneself. Her works have appeared in *Gramercy
Review, Southwest Writers: New Voices, Looking Back to Place,* High
Plains Poetry Society publications, and *The Rag*

Teresa E. Gallion
has published in *Central Avenue, Harwood Review, Broomweed Journal*
and numerous anthologies, including: *Along the Rio Grande, Once Upon
A Place, Book Lung, Earthships* and *Small Canyons 2 Anthology.* She has
a chapbook titled *Walking Sacred Ground (Celebrating the Landscape).*
Writing is a spiritual journey for Teresa.

Patricia Gillikin
is a mom to two amazing people, Alistair and Alex, a writing teacher
at UNM-Valencia campus, and co-organizer, with Erin Northern, of
Albuquerque's OUTSpoken Queer Poetry Slam. She's an utter fangirl
for performance poetry, and takes great delight in watching writers
grow in craft and courage.

Laura Green
wrote her first poem for her first love at fourteen. Since then
her poetry has improved, though sadly, her taste in men has not.
Consequently, she enjoys extended periods of solitude, emerging

occasionally into the social sphere, where you can find her slamming poetry at local coffee shops.

Katrina K. Guarascio
lives in Albuquerque, New Mexico, where she teaches Language Arts, Poetry, and Journalism. Along with numerous literary magazine and ezine publications, she is the author of two chapbooks of poetry, and one book length publication, available through Casa De Snapdragon publishing, entitled *A Scattering of Imperfections.*

Kenneth P. Gurney,
Albuquerque poet, edits the New Mexico poetry anthology *Adobe Walls.* He participates in Albuquerque's poetry scene at open mics and by hosting a poetry salon. His poetry appears on the web and in print regularly. For a full biography, publishing credits and available books visit http://www.kpgurney.me/Poet/Welcome.html

Elene Gusch
has published two poetry chapbooks, *Cosmic Radio* and *The Fine Art of Living in the Past,* but she has been writing mostly prose lately. Some of her yapping about spiritual and social matters can be found at http://elenedom.wordpress.com. You can learn about her Oriental medicine practice at http://kuanyin.elenelistens.com.

Dale Harris
organizes the annual Sunflower Festival Poets & Writers Picnic at the historic Shaffer Hotel in Mountainair , N.M. She is the associate editor of *The Malpais Review* poetry quarterly. From 2002- 2007, she edited *Central Avenue,* a monthly poetry journal and reading series. Her poetry is online at CD Baby.

Beatlick Pamela Adams Hirst
(BA in Communications, *magna cum laude*, Tennessee State) no longer publishes *Beatlick News*. She created Beatlick Press to continue partner Beatlick Joe Speer's work of glorifying the Southwest and publishing talented writers. A free-lance journalist residing in Oaxaca, Mexico, she's investigating alleged dangers of traveling in that country at http://publishingpamela.blogspot.com.

Rev. Rebecca Guile Hudson
is the author of *Out of Cullen Street (A House of Madness)* and *Painted Poems (Portraits of New Mexico)*. She has published in three *Small Canyons* haiku anthologies; *Symphonies*, an anthology of world poetry; *Along The Rio Grande*, poetry from New Mexico; and *The Taj Mahal Review*.

Anthony Hunt
has taught in Nigeria, Maine, Poland, Croatia, Taiwan, and Puerto Rico. His book *Genesis, Structure, and Meaning in Gary Snyder's 'Mountains and Rivers Without End'* was published in 2004. Hunt is completing a novel about Poland, reads regularly at the Church of Beethoven and teaches poetry classes.

Lisa Jacobs
I have been a visual artist for most of my life, but have recently begun writing poetry as part of the process of recreating myself after retirement from an intense day job. I love living in Albuquerque with my husband and some four-legged friends.

Ardith Johnson
always enjoyed poetry but began writing poems only after arriving in Albuquerque in 1988, when she attended Bear Canyon Senior Center (BCSC) writing workshops. She won honorable mention in a BCSC

contest and was published in *The New Mexico Breeze*. "Writing poems added something more to my life."

Kathamann
I've been a painter and sculptor in Santa Fe for thirty years. I am a retired Peace Corps Volunteer/Afghanistan and registered nurse. I have been published in many anthologies and periodicals, including: *Sage Trail, The Rag, Lunarosity, Beatlick News, Small Canyons, Malpai Reviews*, and *Adobe Walls*.

Zachary Kluckman,
an Editor for *Pedestal Magazine* and *The Journal of Truth and Consequence*, also directs Albuquerque's Slam Poet Laureate Program. Founder of the Albuquerque Poetry Festival and a Pushcart Prize nominee with recent publications in *The New York Quarterly, Blue Earth Review*, Kluckman's new book is due out soon.

Sari Krosinsky
edits *Fickle Muses*, an online journal of mythic poetry and fiction. Her poems appear regularly in literary and genre magazines. She received a B.A. in religious studies and M.A. in creative writing from the University of New Mexico. She lives in Albuquerque, N.M., with her partner and cat.

Wayne Lee
teaches at the Institute of American Indian Arts in Santa Fe, NM. His collections include *Doggerel & Caterwauls: Poems Inspired by Cats and Dogs, Twenty Poems from the Blue House* (Whistle Lake Press) and the forthcoming *Vortex* (Red Mountain Press). He is married to poet/painter Alice Lee.

Marietta Patricia Leis
is a visual artist from Albuquerque, New Mexico. Her diverse work includes paintings, drawings, prints and constructions. Her poems often serve in her art installations as text plates. Leis has received many awards and grants, including artist residencies in the U. S. and abroad. www.mariettaleis.com.

Carol Lewis
was born in Chicago, lived in California and now resides in Albuquerque. Poetry surges as blood in her veins. Her poems appear in numerous small poetry magazines and in her chap book, *Unhealed Wound*. She edited/published *the Rag* for six years. She now tutors an ESL student.

Maria Leyba
I am a Chicana poet who resides in Barelas. I carry the *Llanto* (cries) of all women who have inspired and shaped me throughout my lifetime. My madrecita's familia from old Mexico were not only rug weavers but also incredible oral storytellers.

Gina Marselle
is a writer, photographer, teacher, and single mom. She has published work in the *Alibi*, the *Rag*, online with *The Sunday Poem* series, and most recently in *Adobe Walls, an anthology of New Mexico poetry.*

Miranda Marselle
is a youth poet. In January 2010 she became the youngest Fixed and Free featured poet ever. She is also a dancer in the pre-professional program at Keshet Dance Company. She studies flamenco with Casa Flamenca. Finally, she is looking forward to 6th grade in Fall 2011.

Mary McGinnis
has been living, writing, working and laughing in New Mexico since
1972. She has upcoming work in *Adobe Walls* and *The Sow's Ear.* Her
full-length collection, *Listening For Cactus* is still available.

Don McIver
is a former member of the ABQ slam team, author of *The Noisy Pen* and
editor of *A Bigger Poet: The Unlikely Success of the Albuquerque Poetry
Slam Scene.* He's performed all over the United States, produced poetry
events big and small, and been published in numerous magazines and
anthologies.

Merimée Moffitt
arrived in the land of enchantment in 1970. She co-edits *the Rag*, a
monthly broadsheet of poems and co-hosts Dime Stories, a prose
open mic. She has recent work in *Mas Tequila Review 2*, several in
the Sunday Poem on *Duke City Fix*, *Adobe Walls 1 & 2*, and her new
chapbooks.

Samuel Moorman
received his M.A. in Creative Writing from San Francisco State
University in 1995. He currently resides in Albuquerque.

Carol Moscrip
has lived in Albuquerque for 33 years; she has been active in the local
poetry community and has worked as a teacher of writing at the high
school and university levels. Her work has recently appeared in *Adobe
Walls* (2010) and *Beatlick News.*

Yasmeen Najmi
self-published a 2004 poetry chapbook, *Ankh* (Hindi for "Eye"). Her
poems appear in *Kolkata, La Bloga, El Tecolote, Poets for Living Waters*

and anthologies *The Stark Electric Space* and *Adobe Walls.* An environmental planner, her poetry often reflects her deep connection to the ecology and cultures of the Rio Grande.

Bill Nevins

is a cultural journalist, publishing in *Trend, Z, RootsWorld, AbqARTS, Local iQ.* He teaches English at UNM, Valencia Campus. He's made a few films, including *Breakin Blue Burque Brew* and *Committing Poetry in Times of War.* He is on the Poetry Reaper Crew of SAMCROW, in his dreams.

Bruce Noll's

poems are published in journals and magazines such as *Manzanita Quarterly, English Journal, Nebraska Life, The American Entomologist, South Dakota Magazine, JAMA, and ASHA Leader.* For 41 years Noll has presented the works of Walt Whitman in his "PURE GRASS", performed in 26 states and four foreign countries

Mary Oertel-Kirschner

I've been writing poetry most of my life and have met regularly with a group of women poets in Albuquerque for ten years. We published a collection of our work in a chapbook, *Quartet,* in 2003. I've also worked as a news writer, publicist, technical writer, and novelist.

Jill A. Oglesby

lives in Los Lunas with her black labrador Buíochas (Irish for gratitude) and tuxedo cat Binks. She loves summer hiking, dancing, singing, and sitting in sunny windows in winter. She hopes to learn to photosynthesize, make more poems from sloppy real life, propel through crowds like an ammonite, and learn "liminal" in every language.

Marilyn O'Leary
is a retired water lawyer-turned-life coach who has lived in
Albuquerque since 1965. The first poetry she can remember writing
was for Miss Weinschenk's class at West Rockford High School. She
appreciates the encouragement of her poetry group and her husband, a
former teacher of English.

Kate Padilla
is an award-winning and published poet from Socorro, a University
of Wyoming graduate and former journalist. She reviews books
for *AudioFile Magazine* and Authorlink.com, and is a member of
Albuquerque's Word Weavers poetry group. Her writings speak of her
Taos birthplace and growing up in Wyoming.

Scott Palmer
Born in Fort Devens Massachusetts. Father was a military lifer for
twenty-eight years. There was a great measure of pain and destruction
in my childhood. Most of my poetry comes from childhood fragments.
I live to write and I write to live. Poetry saved my life.

Annmarie Pearson
is Chair of Rio Grande Valencia Poets and board member of NM State
Poetry Society. Pearson's poems have appeared in the *Valencia County
News-Bulletin*, University of New Mexico's *Valley Visions*, *New Mexico
Breeze*, Roswell's *Small Canyon 4 Anthology 2009*, and *Playboy Magazine*.
She also completed her first mystery novel.

Charles R. Powell
is a father, grandfather, and retiree who has lived in Albuquerque 25
years. With a BS in Social Science he was a social worker, personnel
representative, and veterans service officer. Charles now spends most
of his time and energy working for justice and world peace.

Robert Arthur Reeves
has been writing poetry since 1965. Check his Website for links to his poetry publications and his partner Sari Krosinsky's:
http://outerchild.wordpress.com

Elizabeth Roll
I find writing poems a way to remember, to communicate, to enliven and to heal. I have lived in Albuquerque for 40 years and raised two children in a bicultural home. I now create poetry with my 6-year-old granddaughter and enjoy sharing my poems.

Bonnie K. Rucobo
earned a B.A. from Reed College in Portland, Oregon, and a J.D. from Golden Gate University in San Francisco, California. She is President of the New Mexico State Poetry Society and has written a novel for middle-grade students to be published in 2011.

Georgia Santa Maria,
a native New Mexican, wrote *The Miami, NM Hippie Mommy Cookbook* and *Lichen Kisses*, a poetry collection, and is writing a novel based on experiences running her great-grandfather's store. Her writing appears in many anthologies, on *Duke City Fix* Sunday Poem and on "Best of" *Duke City Dime Stories* web recordings.

Daniel Schwartz
is a Professor Emeritus and has been teaching for over thirty five years in California, Arizona and New Mexico. He continues to teach part-time in the Sociology Department at the University of New Mexico.

Elaine Schwartz
is a retired college professor and co-founder of Albuquerque Poets Against War. Her poetry, best described as a tapestry of place and

political imagination, has appeared in numerous publications including the *Santa Fe Literary Review, Adobe Walls* and *Malpais Review.*

Lauren Schwartz
has written poetry for over thirty years. She attended the MFA Program at Columbia University in the early 1980s. Her dream of living in New Mexico, writing and photographing here, has been realized after raising 17 year old twin boys in a much more humid place.

Beatlick Joe Speer,
Albuquerque native, edited and published *Beatlick News: Poetry & Arts Newsletter* for 22 years, archived at six American universities. His personal library resides at his beloved New Mexico State University. Joe still inhabits the Internet: writings at www.beatlick.com and recordings at "Beatlick & Beyond" on www.chucksville.com. In January 2011 Beatlick Joe completed his last work, *Backpack Trekker: a 60s Flashback.* Beatlick Joe now treks and writes in an entirely new realm.

Marilyn Stablein's
tenth book *Splitting Hard Ground* won the New Mexico Book Award. Her memoirs include: *Sleeping in Caves* and *Climate of Extremes.* New work is forthcoming in *Kyoto Journal, Sin Fronteras, Mas Tequila Review, Gargoyle* and *Voices of New Mexico.* She teaches Writing Workshops and exhibits assemblages and artist books at Acequia Booksellers.

K. K. (Kitty) Todorovich's
award-winning poems appear in print nationally and internationally. She is a member of the Rio Grande Valencia Chapter of the New Mexico State Poetry Society.

Sal Treppiedi
has two poetry chapbooks: *Random Thoughts of An Obese Mind* (2008) and *Tellin' Tales Out of School* (2010). His work appears in *Earthships: A New Mecca Poetry Collection* and *America Remembered*, an anthology from Virgogray Press. Treppiedi founded Voices Emerging=New Thunder (VE=NT), the New Mexico Middle School Poetry Slam.

Aaron Trumm
was a repeat member of the Albuquerque and Houston (TX) Slam Poetry Teams, and was the number 10 ranked slam poet in America. He also is a musician and owner of NQUIT, a recording company with a studio in Albuquerque. His poetry appears in many chap books and anthologies. www.nquit.com

Bob Warren
I was born and raised in Detroit where over the course of years I was shot at thirteen times—and missed. I began writing poetry in the 8th grade. Married a lady with 5 kids. We're up to 14 grandkids and 8 great-grandkids.

Stewart S. Warren
is the author of ten poetry collections and is published in various journals and anthologies. His poetry is both personal and transpersonal with a mystic undercurrent. Stewart lives in northern New Mexico, "A place," he says, "of resilient, fragile enchantment." www.heartlink.com

Richard Wolfson
began writing poetry after the death of his wife JoAnn, a poet, in 2004. Many of these poems come from dreams and shamanic journeys. He currently lives in Albuquerque with his second wife Vicki Bolen, an artist who collaborates with him on books, cards, and prints.

Jason Yurcic
was born while his father was in prison (and later was murdered).
Jason learned street-smarts at his grandfather's junkyard. A collegiate
football player and professional boxer, Jason became disillusioned with
violence. His published poetry books include: *Voice of My Heart, Word
Son, Poems by Jason L. Yurcic,* and *Odes to Anger.*

www.ingramcontent.com/pod-product-compliance
Lightning Source LLC
Chambersburg PA
CBHW051831090426
42736CB00011B/1747